# **when**anger **scares**you

## How to Overcome Your Fear of Conflict & Express Your Anger in Healthy Ways

## JOHN R. LYNCH, PH.D.

New Harbinger Publications, Inc.

## Publisher's Note

*This publication is designed to provide accurate and authoritative information in regard to the subject matter covered. It is sold with the understanding that the publisher is not engaged in rendering psychological, financial, legal, or other professional services. If expert assistance or counseling is needed, the services of a competent professional should be sought.*

Distributed in Canada by Raincoast Books.

Copyright © 2004 by John R. Lynch, Ph.D.
New Harbinger Publications, Inc.
5674 Shattuck Avenue
Oakland, CA 94609

Cover design by Amy Shoup
Edited by Brady Kahn
Text design by Tracy Marie Carlson

ISBN 1-57224-347-3 Paperback

New Harbinger Publications' Web site address: www.newharbinger.com

06    05    04

10    9    8    7    6    5    4    3    2    1

First printing

This book is dedicated to my mother, Clare Ann Norris, who passed to the next life during the writing of this book, leaving this world a better place than she found it. She was our mother, grandmother, wife, sister, and friend. And she was always a lady.

# contents

# acknowledgments

I want to acknowledge the helpful reactions and comments from the editors at New Harbinger, especially Catharine Sutker, Carole Honeychurch, and Brady Kahn, whose thoughtful responses helped me shape and make clear the thoughts presented here.

I want to acknowledge my family's support and understanding for the time taken away from family time to write this manuscript. I want to especially thank my wife, Mary Polce-Lynch, for her help through talks and sharing ideas that became parts of these chapters, especially her generous help with the material in chapter 4.

I want to thank Janice Mallory, Susan Pleasants, and Mary Polce-Lynch for their help in the production of this manuscript. I want to mention and thank Lisa Hill O'Shea and my daughter, Kathryn Lynch, for reading an early edition of the manuscript and for her helpful comments and reactions. I am grateful to my good friend and esteemed colleague, Chris Kilmartin, Ph.D., for his valuable contribution to this book.

Finally, and mostly, I want to thank and acknowledge my clients, who have taught me so much and have honored me by letting me into their lives to see, feel, and understand the conflicts they experience. Their struggles bring the real human face to what would otherwise be an intellectual exercise.

# preface

I am writing this book to address the issues of anger avoiders because I am moved by their struggles and troubles. In my work as a clinical psychologist, I recognize the toll anger avoidance takes on individuals and the problems it causes in relationships. Anger avoiders are good-hearted, well-intentioned people who would rather suffer personal distress than cause distress in others. I am writing this book to name a problem that plagues many people and to give them hope.

I am writing this book for laypeople and professionals, to propose a model for understanding anger that will lead to constructive resolutions. Anger is both an important and a terribly misunderstood feeling. Anger and fear of rage are at the core of many of the personal and relationship difficulties people face. Yet how people look at these feelings can lead to healthy or unhealthy interactions. My cognitive model helps people be in charge of the decisions and behaviors they engage in. If we change the way we think about interactions, our behavior, reactions, and the outcomes can change too.

Anger is also a cultural dilemma. We cannot fully understand or hope to change the patterns that trap anger avoiders unless we understand the full context in which these problems arise. We grow up in a world where it's bad to lose control, where "becoming angry" is the same as losing control. When we see violence on television, in the news, or in fictional dramas, or read newspaper accounts of crimes and violence, we can easily get the wrong message about anger, for assailants are frequently described as "angry." Thus we perpetuate the patterns of anger avoidance. This awareness has strengthened my resolve to write this book, and helped me become more determined to put a human face on the problems that anger avoiders experience.

This book is not a scholarly treatise. It is based on my experience with people, not on statistics or researched treatment protocols. The cases of anger avoiders are grounded in actual cases—my own or those of other therapists. Places, names, ages, occupations, and personal characteristics have been changed to preserve individual privacy.

# 1

# anger avoiders, anger exploders, and healthy anger expressers

Cassandra had a lot to do that day, while the cashier talked incessantly to a friend instead of ringing up her items. Cassandra was fuming on the inside, but when the cashier finally looked up and said, "Hi, how are you?" Cassandra replied, "Fine, thanks. How are you?"

Jim played softball every Tuesday night in the summers. It was his only night out with the guys. One evening his wife didn't get home on time to take over with the kids so he could get to the game. She sensed something was amiss and asked, "What's wrong?" He replied, "Oh, nothing," took a shower, and went to bed.

Betty liked her job but didn't like her coworker. Betty worked hard and watched as her coworker came in late and left early every day. Betty's supervisor noticed a change in Betty's usual cheerful disposition and asked what was bothering her. Betty replied that she was just having a bad day.

Lamar arrived at the doctor's office on time. Two people who arrived after Lamar saw the doctor before he was called back by the nurse. Lamar could feel his blood pressure rise, but he greeted the nurse with a blunted "hello."

Do these stories sound familiar to you? Cassandra, Jim, Betty, and Lamar are *anger avoiders*. They avoid conflict, confrontation, and expressions of anger. As anger avoiders, they are more than uncomfortable with anger. They avoid, deny, or repress it. If you ask them why they behave this way, they will defend or excuse their actions, or lack of action, with a rationale that makes sense to them. You would hear:

✦ "I don't want to be rude."

✦ "I don't want to hurt someone's feelings."

✦ "I don't want to lose control."

✦ "I don't want to feel bad."

✦ "I don't want to be seen by others as an unlikable person."

Whatever their reasons, each of these people has a long-term pattern of avoiding anger and conflict. These people are afraid of their own anger and other people's anger as well. As a result, they lose the chance to solve problems, express themselves, and experience a richer life. This happens because they do not see anger as a message indicating that they feel threatened in some way, because they get confused and disorganized by the experience of feeling aroused by anger, and because they lack the skills needed to express anger in healthy ways. I will elaborate on these three themes shortly, but first, let's see if your life is affected by how you handle and express anger.

# Do You Have Difficulty with Anger?

Perhaps you're wondering if you are an anger avoider. Being an anger avoider is not uncommon. Anger is a feeling a lot of people have trouble with. Anger has acquired a bad name over time and has been associated with everything from a shameful loss of control to outright violence. But anger is simply nature's way of saying that there's a problem that needs solving. This book will cover more about what anger is and what it's not supposed to be later. For right now, see if you have difficulties expressing anger. Take a look at these next questions and see how many you might answer yes to. Do you

+ Deliberately avoid conflict with people, keeping your feelings and thoughts to yourself instead?

+ Seek approval and consensus instead of stating your real thoughts on an issue?

+ Fear that you'll yell, scream, or lose control when you feel angry, so you hold it in or deny your feelings instead?

+ Fear that you're a bad person when you get angry?

+ Get so uncomfortable expressing anger that you don't express it?

+ Fear that other people will think badly of you if you express your anger, so you withhold it?

+ Remain polite and say "nothing's wrong" when you are angry about something?

+ Become so concerned about hurting your spouse's feelings that you never say what's bothering you?

+ Find yourself making excuses for other people's behavior when it angers you, such as, "He probably didn't mean that," instead of dealing directly with the person?

+ Try to be a team player and go along with people even when you see a better but unpopular approach?

+ Experience a lot of physical or emotional pain when there is a lot of stress in your life?

+ Feel flushed, turn red, sweat, or begin to hyperventilate when you are angry?

+ Lose control and yell, later regretting it and promising to never lose control again?

✓✦ Lose or harm relationships by the way you express or avoid expressing your anger?

✓✦ See your family doctor on a regular basis for aches and pains that have no medical origin?

✦ Come from a family where anger was expressed violently or was never expressed at all?

✓✦ Have chronic low self-esteem?

✓✦ Experience frequent bouts of anxiety without knowing what you are anxious about?

✓✦ Feel like you are underperforming at work, that your talents and skills aren't being fully utilized?

✓✦ Frequently feel depressed, usually without a clear or recent reason for feeling this way?

Did you answer a lot of these questions with a yes? If so, you may be an anger avoider. What does it mean to be an anger avoider? And, if you are an anger avoider, is there hope? Anger avoiders are people who avoid, deny, or repress anger in themselves or others. As you will see, there are logical reasons for feeling uncomfortable or even afraid of anger, and logical solutions to the problem as well. Anger avoiders usually have misconceptions about anger. These misconceptions lead to a style of behaving that does not allow them to develop good anger expression skills. Lacking expressive skills, anger avoiders experience depression, anxiety, low self-esteem, and other limitations and discomforts. If you are an anger avoider, this book will help you to develop new and adaptive anger expression skills.

# Common Misconceptions

When you think of anger, what comes to mind? Like many people, you might conjure up images of violence, broken relationships, hurt feelings, or feeling bad about yourself. For many people, just thinking about anger feels uncomfortable. Because we often associate anger with a loss of control, or even aggression, we learn messages such as: anger hurts people, anger is violent, you are bad or doing something wrong if you are angry, people won't like you if you are angry, and, most of all, don't be angry!

Simply put, we mistakenly learn that good people do not get angry and that getting angry means behaving badly or feeling bad. Many people need anger management classes to control anger. They are *anger exploders*. Many, however, avoid expressions of anger for fear of being an anger exploder or being seen in an unfavorable light. These people need a different kind of anger management because they avoid anger. Anger exploders are loud, easily noticed, and can create significant suffering in others. Most anger avoiders, however, suffer silently, invisibly, and alone.

This book is written for you if you chronically avoid conflict and confrontation and suffer from this avoidance in occupational settings, in personal relationships, and in terms of your self-esteem. Anger avoiders are polite, quiet, and distressed. They are competent but feel inept. They are compassionate, yet they fear being mean. They experience a different face of anger—not the loud, explosive one that hurts others. Their anger hurts themselves. Anger avoiders live in the shadow of anger. If you're an anger avoider, your fear of anger colors everything you do. See if you recognize yourself in the stories below.

## ✦ Bob's Story

Bob was recently promoted in his department to director of human resources. He worked hard, listened well, wanted to help people, and showed an ability to get difficult jobs done correctly. In short, he was a competent professional. But he felt quite threatened in his new position. One of his secretaries was not doing her job. She was well liked by her peers and had been in her position much longer than Bob had been in his. Still, she made personal calls on the job, was slow and inattentive in her work, and made numerous clerical errors on Bob's reports. Bob feared her performance reflected poorly on him, but Bob avoided the problem and did not correct her. He wondered if he was up to the job. He had trouble sleeping and was gulping Maalox like it was candy. Bob became afraid his superiors would see him as an ineffectual leader. When friends asked why he didn't talk directly with her, he fumbled a bit and said, "I'm afraid I'll get angry, lose control, and yell at her." He added, "I don't know what to say and I didn't want to come across as a mean boss." He also reluctantly

admitted that he was afraid she would not like him
if he expressed displeasure about her performance.
Not surprisingly, Bob's father had been a very angry
man who was violent on occasion, and his behavior
left Bob feeling bad about himself when he was a
child. Bob associated his father's violent behavior with
expressions of anger. So Bob had learned to avoid
being angry. Unfortunately, he also avoided facing or
solving problems.

## ✦ Salinda's Story

Salinda was employed as a financial manager, and after
twenty years, she had proven her professional abilities.
None of her friends knew that she was on the verge of
bankruptcy, and they would have been shocked to hear
it. She was so successful and responsible. But Salinda
was also very depressed. Her husband loved to golf
and to travel and to buy the best of everything. His
spending had landed them $40,000 in debt, and they
were in danger of losing the house. Salinda felt
anxious and became unsure of decisions at work and
at home. How had she let this happen? She handled
confrontations at work without a worry. Yet she was
afraid of confronting her husband. She had kept
hoping he'd just "get it" and change his spending
habits. But the problems kept spinning out of control.
So did Salinda. Her marriage became more strained.
She didn't feel close to her husband. She avoided
talking with him and withdrew into herself. After a
while, they were more like roommates than husband
and wife. Salinda felt bad about not being a better wife,
and guilty about not wanting to be intimate with her
husband. She couldn't understand what was happening
to her marriage and her life. Salinda felt doubtful
of herself and behaved in ways that left her feeling
more doubtful. She knew she was capable of addressing
problems directly and effectively, but somehow she
left those skills at work.

Bob and Salinda are anger avoiders. Their anger is below the surface, often unrecognized even by themselves. Anger, especially in
its seeming absence, influences all aspects of their lives. Secretly,

both fear they would explode or would somehow feel badly about themselves if they confronted conflict. They think anger can only be hurtful, destructive, or shameful, and their fear of anger hinders them. They never learned that anger is a natural call to solve a problem, an energy to be used constructively. As a result, Bob and Salinda are not free to address and solve problems. Bob and Salinda feel troubled and trapped. Their way of avoiding anger hurts them as much as they fear their anger would hurt others.

## Common Characteristics

Anger avoiders share several characteristics. First, they assume anger is a bad feeling to have, and that only bad things come from anger—that if you are angry, you will either act badly or feel bad for feeling angry. It is as if expressing anger can only mean yelling, losing control, or becoming "a bad person." Anger avoiders assume that good people don't get angry.

Second, ironically, they usually do not feel anger. Rather, they feel fear of anger. Or at least what they call anger. As you will soon see, they actually fear rage. Fear, however, leads them to develop deferential and avoidance behaviors. As a result, they do not resolve conflicts in a fair and balanced way. Instead they ignore their own needs and chronically give in, rather then address problems head-on. Frequently this results in chronic depression, intense anxiety, low self-esteem, and a variety of other symptoms. These people do not need traditional anger management approaches, which seek to contain the expression of anger. They need a way to align with their anger, not against it, and to express anger safely and constructively.

Third, anger avoiders are typically sensitive and compassionate and thus do not want to hurt anyone. So they resolve never to be violent and destructive, mean, or hurtful. Fearing that anger is bad, they simply avoid it. Most often, anger avoiders grew up either with anger exploders or with overly polite anger avoiders. They learned to associate anger with a shameful and dangerous loss of control or with "being bad." Even more, they learned to anticipate that anger could only hurt people.

Finally, anger avoiders share misconceptions about the meaning and value of anger. The problems anger avoiders experience are often in relationships, but it isn't their misconceptions about relationships that is the problem. It is their misconceptions about anger that is the problem. It is in their relationships with other people that anger avoiders manifest their misconceptions about anger.

# Conflict and Its Relationship to Anger

Conflict occurs when two opinions, desires, or needs collide. Conflict can help you clarify and strengthen your views and values, and help you develop trust in relationships. Anger avoiders do not solve problems that involve conflict or confrontation, however. They know how it feels to be on the receiving end of what they learned to call "anger," and they would rather feel hurt and cheated than risk hurting someone else. Their empathic, caring, and compassionate traits do not help them, though. They withdraw, give in, and ignore and avoid conflict, and since they think that anger is synonymous with conflict, they avoid anger as well. They consider both to be destructive. As a result, their relationships become very limited, and, despite being quite competent, they never fully develop leadership skills or take adversarial positions. As a rule, anger avoiders seek consensus over conflict and cooperation over competition. Depending on the demands of a situation, consensus and cooperation may produce the best outcomes. But to avoid conflict and competition as an overarching pattern results in avoiding strength, clarity, and empowerment.

### ✦ Kathy's Story

Kathy's life was in complete disarray. She was overweight, had high blood pressure, and couldn't manage to get up most mornings. She dreaded another day of dealing with people in her life. People meant to demands. Other people's demands became Kathy's obligations. She was married with two kids and had a lot of obligations of her own. Yet she drove her elderly father everywhere, even though her brother and sister were nearby and unmarried. She frequently missed lunches with friends because of her father's constant needs. This made her very mad, but she told no one. Her father complained to Kathy about every concern, whim, or problem he faced. Somehow Kathy felt she had to sit and listen to him, whether or not she wanted to or even had the time to listen. Meanwhile, Kathy's adult nephew, who lived with them, ran up her phone bills even though he had no income to pay for them. Kathy found out, but never asked him to pay. She couldn't bring herself to talk with him about this uncomfortable topic. It was as if Kathy had no will of her own. Instead, the demands and expectations of others seemed to rule her life. To Kathy, this was normal life. It had always been this way.

In other times, Kathy would have been labeled "codependent." She would have been encouraged to take assertiveness training and learn to stand up for herself. Yet that would not have solved the problem Kathy experienced. Kathy feared conflict because it had always meant one thing: violence. Kathy feared that becoming assertive could only lead to physical aggression on someone's part. Kathy feared the physical feelings that welled up in her when her father asked yet another favor. Kathy felt these feelings could only lead to the same violent and hurtful explosions she witnessed and experienced as a child. She knew no other outcome and had no other experience, so she complied. It was the best alternative available to her.

Kathy is a person who does not know her own strength because she is constantly cooperative and polite. She has lost awareness of her anger, and in doing so, has lost access to her strength and abilities to effectively solve problems and take care of herself.

Kathy fears that exploding would be her only recourse if she let herself become angry. Actually, Kathy knows very little about anger because what she has experience with and avoids is actually rage. A healthy expression of anger is not the midpoint between avoiding and exploding. Rather, healthy anger expression reflects an entirely different understanding about anger, a developed set of skills, and an integration of strong feelings with a well-formulated goal. Healthy anger expressers do not fear or avoid or explode. They step into anger and use it as a messenger that there is a problem to solve and as a tool with which to solve the problem. Kathy, however, fears she'll explode and be just like the parents she swore to be different from. Without healthy anger expression skills, Kathy's options are limited.

## Healthy Anger Expressers

Interestingly, healthy *anger expressers* possess the same qualities of empathy, caring, and compassion that anger avoiders
possess, but healthy anger expressers communicate anger in productive and effective ways. They feel the confidence and empowerment that anger avoiders lack because they understand and
trust themselves to assess situations, and to act constructively.
Healthy anger expressers trust that conflict can strengthen relationships when both individuals are open and honest about the
conflict. Expressing anger is telling the truth and dealing directly
with real problems. When partners know that each will name
problems in a constructive and respectful manner and will
resolve to solve them, their relationship becomes safer and stronger. Healthy anger expressers know themselves and their partners, and are familiar with healthy, even vigorous and intense,
interactions. They are comfortable in positions of authority and
responsibility because they know how to be fair to themselves
and to others at the same time. Anger expressers can be firm *and*
gentle, decisive *and* compassionate. They do not worry about hurting others with their anger because they know anger is a messenger, alerting us that there is a problem that needs our attention.

## The Importance of Names

Names are important because they organize how we understand ourselves and our world. What we name things shapes our
expectations and reactions to those things. Bob and Salinda name
themselves weak, inept, and incompetent. They understand themselves and their behavior in light of these names and secretly feel
ashamed of themselves, which contributes to self-doubt, fear, and
more avoidance. Names produce self-fulfilling prophecies. If Bob
and Salinda named themselves anger avoiders, their behavior
would actually make more sense. It isn't really anger or even
conflict that they avoid. It is the destructiveness and discomfort
that they equate with anger.

When they name themselves weak, inept, or incompetent,
they behave in ways that produce negative outcomes. If Bob and
Salinda named themselves compassionate and well-intentioned,
they would achieve better outcomes. And they would have even
more options for effective behaviors and reactions if they integrated their good intentions with healthy expressive skills and

became healthy anger expressers. Bob and Salinda can learn to be healthy anger expressers. Naming themselves anger avoiders is a start.

The importance of names is illustrated by the story of the three umpires who are asked to describe how they perform their job. The first umpire says, "There are balls and there are strikes, and I call them as I see them." The second umpire says, "There are balls and there are strikes, and I call them as they are." The third umpire says, "There are balls and there are strikes, but they aren't anything until I call them." Which umpire do you think is the wisest of the three? The third umpire understood the power, importance, and effect of properly naming things. What you name things determines how you feel and respond. This theme will be elaborated upon in chapter 2. But, as you can see, if you name anger as a constructive energy used to solve problems, and you name rage as a destructive energy, then you would no longer avoid anger. And you would more effectively avoid rageful outbursts. Naming feelings, expectations, and assumptions can clarify your responses and your behavior. The goal of this book is to destigmatize anger and help anger avoiders develop into healthy anger expressers.

# Anger and Emotional Education

Anger is arguably the most difficult feeling to understand or manage. Yet it is only one of many feelings we have. But many of us do not know what our feelings are or what to do with the feelings we have. We go to school to learn how to solve math problems and how to comprehend concepts from basic logic to obscure poetry and philosophy. We can learn skills in school to help us become carpenters, computer programmers, or cosmetologists. But what about our emotional education? No matter where our other skills have taken us, we have to deal with the emotions of everyday life.

For help in interpreting and responding to our emotional reality, we need what's called *affective education*. Affective education teaches us what feelings mean and what they don't mean, how we can grow with our feelings, how our feelings can help us understand ourselves and our unique needs in life, and especially how best to handle and express our feelings. This book is an attempt to add to affective education for adults by addressing the role of anger, especially as it functions in adult relationships at home and at work.

Without accurate or helpful information about feelings, it's natural to fill in the gaps with fears and insecurities. You may distort the meanings of your feelings. Your fears about your feelings may limit your perspective about what should happen or what it all means. Then you may react to feelings in misguided ways and end up creating additional and unnecessary problems.

Anger avoiders develop problems because of specific, understandable, and therefore correctable reasons. Like many people, anger avoiders can become confused and disorganized by aroused feelings. Perhaps this confusion describes some of the difficulties you experience. You don't have to continue to live with misguided assumptions about feelings and suffer with the limitations that result. This book is intended to help you name the origins of some of your problems with anger, especially in relationships, and it offers a cognitive model to organize your understanding of and response to anger.

## The Larger Problem with Anger

Discomfort and distortions about anger are both a personal and a cultural dynamic. Personal problems occur in a cultural context, and consistent personal problems occur with cultural support. Anger has a bad name in the larger American culture. It is associated with a shameful loss of control and composure. Largely unspoken cultural standards inhibit a healthy and impassioned expression of anger as a normal experience of living. In American culture, anger implies a lack of respect and the breakup, or ending, of a relationship. It implies alienation, rejection, and humiliation. Anger implies a lack of control, and lack of control is  shameful. Somehow we are supposed to be in control. The subtle and unnamed affective education the culture provides teaches people to fear and avoid anger, with varying results. It would not be surprising to find a person with an Italian background to have more comfort with passionate expressions of feelings than a person with a British "stiff upper lip." It would not be surprising to find that a person from a rough neighborhood might be more familiar with a range of anger expressions and meanings than a person from a very polite, well-to-do neighborhood. Distorted assumptions and teachings about anger are both a personal and cultural phenomenon. A healthy model of anger can have immediate personal effects, and hopefully, in time, change cultural assumptions and limitations about anger.

# How to Use This Book

You are beginning a journey of change. Some of the first things that may change are your ideas about anger, but it takes time and effort to translate a change in ideas to a change in behavior and relationships. Real change takes time, especially when it involves ingrained patterns like those described in this book. To facilitate making changes in your life, you may find it helpful to think of each chapter in this book as a stage of change. Each chapter will introduce a new idea, or one small step. Chapter 1 has already introduced the idea that anger avoiders share misconceptions about anger and therefore avoid it. Chapter 2 begins the change process by characterizing anger as a constructive response to a threat and rage as a destructive response. Chapters 3 and 4 investigate the range of symptoms that result from suppressing your anger. Chapter 3 describes how feelings actually do not create problems, but feelings *about* feelings, such as feeling afraid of feeling anger or feeling ashamed of feeling sad, create problems. Chapter 4 introduces the idea that we have a mind in our body that experiences anger in a physiological manner. You'll learn that anger is both a psychological and physical experience, and changing your behavior will involve both psychological and physical awareness. Chapter 5 introduces the term *psychological air* to describe how we acquire the messages we take in when we first learn how to be ourselves in our family of origin; problems with anger begin with the messages we receive in our families and other formative relationships. Chapter 6 describes the internal, subjective experience of anger avoiders. Chapter 7 describes a sequence of interventions to develop healthy anger expression skills. You will learn how healthy anger expressers do it, and how you can do it too. Finally, you'll learn about how anger presents unique difficulties for women and for men, and what women and men can do to develop better relationship and anger expression skills. Chapter 8 describes the particular problems with anger faced by women and chapter 9 covers the problems men face with anger. Chapter 10 is about the long-term process of changing behavior and interaction habits.

Each chapter introduces a new idea for you to think about. Each chapter will add to the change process, bit by bit, and step by step. This book also includes two writing exercises designed to help you realize and solidify the changes you are making along the way. Both exercises are described here. You can begin to use them now and at the end of each chapter. You may find that you have less to write about now, since you are just beginning this change process. Don't worry. There will be more to write about as you continue reading.

The first writing exercise is to keep a journal, and as you come upon an idea that is new or different, jot it down. Note how the idea applies to you. Write down new ideas and old ideas that are rekindled by what you've read. See which ideas are most absent or present in your life, and which ideas bother you the most or have hindered you the most.

The second writing exercise is more detailed and sequenced. I learned this exercise from a workshop given by Cory Hammonds, Ph.D., for survivors of severe and repeated trauma (Hammonds 1992). I have adapted his work for use with a variety of problems, including anger and other confused feelings. I often ask my clients to do this exercise to help make behavioral changes more real, immediate, and stable.

1. First, you write down what caused you to acquire or believe the particular misconception you have been following. For instance, this could be a couple of sentences about how you assumed anger meant yelling because that's what your father did and your mother called it anger by saying, "Leave him alone when he's angry." Maybe you thought that anger is expressed by yelling, and you learned that if you are not yelling, then you are successfully not being angry. You might write:

✦ "I learned to fear my father's rage and came to fear my own anger as an adult."

✦ "I learned that anger meant being violent, so I always feared becoming violent."

✦ "I could feel the tension in my father's body before he hit me, and I learned to fear the tension in my body when I'm angry."

✦ "My family was horrified when I expressed normal anger as a child, and I've learned to be ashamed of my own feelings."

✦ "Every time my parents yelled at me, they lost control and screamed or hit me, and I learned that way of parenting my kids as well."

2. Second, you write about how this misconception has hurt, hindered, or affected your life so far. You might write about how you yelled at intimate partners and hurt their feelings or damaged the relationships. You could write about how you found people who yelled just like your father did, or how you've quietly avoided conflicts for fear that you'd yell or for fear that the other person would think poorly of you. For instance, you might write:

✦ "I have always avoided standing up for myself, and have been walked on by several people, and felt very hurt and used."

✦ "I have missed several opportunities to move ahead in my career because I was afraid of the conflict I had to face."

✦ "I have stayed in poor relationships because I didn't want to hurt the other person, but it ended up hurting me to stay."

✦ "I have suffered with depression and anxiety because of how I learned to stuff my real feelings."

✦ "I have not become the person I could be, because I am afraid that other people will not like me if I state my own opinions."

3. Third, you write about how your behavior will change with a new idea. Begin each sentence in this section with "From now on, I will . . ." You might write:

✦ "From now on, I will stand up for myself and not allow people to yell at me."

✦ "From now on, I will speak my mind in a way that is respectful to myself and to whomever I am talking to."

✦ "From now on, I am going to slow down and think my way through each day at work, instead of just trying to be nice all the time."

✦ "From now on, I will be sure that I'm being truthful with my feelings before I begin to talk with someone else."

✦ "From now on, I will make my point clear without making the issue clouded by screaming."

✦ "From now on, I will parent my kids in a healthy way and help them grow up to feel good about themselves."

✦ "From now on, I will be proud of the feelings I have and express them in respectful ways."

When you've finished the three parts of this exercise, you might want to read your responses out loud. Saying them aloud helps the ideas come to life.

## Overcoming Anger Avoidance

Anger avoidance is a problem. It affects not only the anger avoider. It is a problem that affects all people in relationships with anger avoiders. Relationships suffer or are limited, and work productivity or career development can be compromised. But like many problems, this problem has a solution. Naming the problem is the first step toward a solution, so you are already getting better.

Chapter 2 introduces a model for understanding anger that will help you understand the problem of anger avoidance and see the possibilities for different outcomes. This model will help clarify the original and intended meanings of anger, rage, and fear. Later chapters will look at the symptoms anger avoiders experience and the physical manifestations of anger that can feel frightening and lead to rageful responses. You will also see how anger avoiders, based on their experience, would naturally make the assumption that anger can only be violent and destructive.

## Changing Your Beliefs and Behaviors

So, take out your journal. Make a list of the ideas in this chapter that are new to you. Make a list of the ideas that you previously had but may have been stimulated by reading this chapter.

1. Which ideas are most applicable to your life today?

2. Which ideas are related to problems you face today?

3. Which problems are easiest to change?

4. Which ones are hardest?

# 2

# recognizing your emotions: separating anger and rage

Anger and rage sometimes confuse people, and they get mislabeled. They have numerous similarities and very important differences. Both have the same origins. They are triggered by events that occur in people's lives. Physically, they can feel the same, bringing flushed skin, rapid heart beats, trembling muscles, or other physical sensations. Both have the same purpose. Anger and rage are nature's way of providing us with energy to protect ourselves when confronted with a threat; this is commonly referred to as the *fight-or-flight response*.

Anger and rage are different in the outcomes they each produce. You act in anger when you constructively solve problems in your life. You act in rage when you destructively solve problems. Anger is a constructive energy. Rage is a destructive energy. Identifying and naming these differences is critical to understanding anger and rage and changing your coping mechanisms. Without accurately naming feelings, you operate on assumptions and habit. If you have come to assume that anger is mean-spirited, violent, out of control, or shameful, as many people have, then you will avoid anger—not because anger is destructive, but because you assume it is destructive. You will habitually avoid conflict when you feel angry, because you assume anger makes an interaction dangerous. You unconsciously named anger as an undesirable feeling and then avoided expressions of anger because of what you assume will be undesirable outcomes. But if you named anger as an impassioned but well-thought-out problem-solving energy, you would behave differently. Naming a feeling leads to action appropriate to that feeling.

Feelings become what you call them. Take Jane's story. Jane appeared fearful, tearful, and distraught. She had missed two weeks of work and was afraid she was falling apart and would be unable to recover. She said to her therapist, "I'm depressed." Her therapist asked why. She said, "My father recently died and I miss him." Jane named herself "depressed." She assumed she was doing something wrong and should be on medication. Her therapist said, "Jane, it sounds like you are sad. You miss your dad." Jane let tears run down her cheeks unchecked. She looked relieved. "I am sad," she said in agreement and recognition, and cried freely. When Jane labeled her feelings "depressed" she acted depressed and thought of herself as depressed. Since depression is a disorder, she assumed it was bad to be depressed and thought she should take medication to fix it. Naming the feeling properly helped her understand and move into the feeling. Jane was able to begin to grieve her father's death, holding on to the qualities she admired in him, and eventually to move on with her life.

# Feelings and Names

How you label feelings is important. In fact, labeling anything plays a very large role in how you think, feel, or react. For instance, picture in your mind a person described as loud, red-faced, and gesturing wildly. Notice what you think about this person. How do you feel when you picture the person in your mind? How would you react if you saw this person walk toward you? Now picture a person described as passionate, intensely focused, and driven to action. What do you think when you imagine this person? How do you feel when you picture this person in your mind? And how would you react if you saw this person walking toward you?

The words used to describe these two people act as labels. Labels have meaning and shape how you think, feel, and react.

They influence what you expect to happen. Was the first person safe? Would you feel at ease with this person, or would you feel on your guard and uneasy? How about the second person? Was that person safe? Would you feel at ease or on your guard? Which person would you most likely laugh and feel comfortable with? Which one would you tolerate mistakes with?

Labels are important. They shape your assumptions, your sense of safety, your thoughts, feelings, and expectations. In the above example, these labels are even more telling when you realize that these are two descriptions of the same person. It wasn't the person you reacted to as much as it was the descriptions, or labels. What you call things determines to a large degree what they mean to you. Similarly, identifying and naming feelings can have powerful implications. In many ways, feelings become what they are called. Labeling leads you to comply with the label rather than to be open to reality.

## Utilizing Names

Medical doctors know the importance of utilizing names. When you undergo a medical procedure, a doctor rarely tells you, "This will hurt." Instead he or she says, "You will feel pressure," or "You may experience some discomfort in this area." And in fact, this is what happens. You experience "discomfort" or "pressure." If the doctor said, "This will hurt like hell," then that's what you would feel. Doctors create a cognitive understanding or perception of the experience you will feel. They name the feeling for you. Then you feel the feeling you were expecting. And it works! Instead of your fear and anxiety distorting the sensation and magnifying it into frightening pain, the doctor helps you anticipate "discomfort." In subtle ways you do what you'd expect to do when you feel discomfort. You tolerate it. By creating this expectation, the actual experience makes more sense and is organized in a way that allows you to use your perceptions and your cognitive abilities to manage the experience. You may say to yourself, "I can tolerate this discomfort," or "This pressure will only last a short while." Without a frame of reference, you may tend to be startled, get disorganized, and overreact with fear or panic to initial physical and psychological arousal. The more you know what to expect and why you would feel the sensations you feel, the better you can manage the event.

Reacting to angry feelings works similarly. If anger is named as something that is dangerous and violent, then when you feel strong physiological arousal (flushed skin, rapid breathing, dilated pupils), you may fear you will explode into violent behavior. So you avoid the feeling instead. If anger could be associated with honest problem solving, then the same strong physiological arousal would signal you to use all your personal and relational skills to address and solve a real problem with the important people in your life.

Later, this chapter will present a model for understanding anger. The model outlines the differences between anger and rage. It is designed to help you change your behavior by knowing what to expect from your feelings.

Of course, understanding the differences between anger and rage is quite different from experiencing intense feelings in the moment. Developing a model is a cognitive experience (having a thought), and having intense feelings is an affective experience (experiencing strong feelings) with physical manifestations (flushed skin, rapid heartbeat and breathing). The value of developing a model for understanding anger, rage, and fear is this: If you understand what is supposed to happen, and what goes wrong in interactions with others, you will have a better chance of correcting the problem. If, in nonemotional moments, you can name feelings and plan to manage these feelings by developing better responses and expressions, then in the affective and physical moment, you will be able to carry out your plan. That's the goal. In other words, think and plan first. Then when you get upset, follow the directions.

# Anger and Rage

Again, people often mislabel anger and rage and don't even discriminate between the two, but call both "anger." You may associate anger with all the negative qualities of rage. This would lead you to think, feel, and react to anger as if it were something undesirable, something you feel afraid or ashamed of, and something you react to by avoiding or denying. Wow! Labels are important!

This chapter will show you the differences between anger and rage, and how to begin the process of changing both your response to anger and your behavioral responses to conflict. Here are some basic definitions of anger and rage that will help to organize your thinking about them.

## Knowing the Difference

Anger and rage, in spite of seeming so similar, are very different from each other. Acting in anger, you produce constructive outcomes, while rageful actions produce destructive outcomes. In other words, anger can be a constructive energy if you handle your feelings in an organized manner. Rage can be destructive when you don't. This difference is not always evident. It is not uncommon to hear the news media describe an assailant as angry and upset over a domestic dispute, or someone on a shooting spree at a former workplace as feeling angry about being fired. "If that's anger," many people often conclude, "I will avoid expressions of anger!" Yet these behaviors aren't angry at all. They are rageful. "Anger" has been used so generally that it can mean a range of reactions, from battering a spouse and children to telling a coworker you will stop covering up for his tardiness because it doubles your workload. Using the same word to describe these two situations renders it relatively meaningless.

Again, anger and rage have important similarities and even more important differences. Anger and rage are both natural responses to a threat. Neither can occur without a threat. Anger and rage are similar in that they both represent a response to a threat. Both anger and rage have a purpose. They provide you with energy to protect yourself. But, the method for each differs. Angry responses protect you by developing a constructive solution to a problem. Rage responses protect you by destroying or eliminating the source of the threat.

In relationships, healthy angry responses produce a win-win situation. Both people benefit when problems in the relationship are solved in a way that respects each person. Rage produces a winner and a loser. The winner feels artificially safe and the loser feels unsafe and frightened, hurt physically or emotionally, shamed, or otherwise silenced. The relationship is harmed as a result. The "winner" is only safe because the relationship is harmed.

In a few pages you will see a five-part cognitive model for understanding both anger and rage and for developing healthy ways to express anger. Before that, it would be helpful to develop a better understanding of how anger and rage are linked and why you need to deal with them in an organized manner. Here is a simple diagram that shows the sequence of events that ultimately leads to an expression of anger or rage. Anger and rage are outcomes of a process that is triggered by threats and is all about responding to those threats with the goal of protecting yourself.

That you will respond is a given. How you respond is open to many healthy and unhealthy possibilities. This book is about learning how you respond to threats now, understanding that *not* responding is a response, and learning how to respond to threats in a healthy and effective manner.

Event

↓

Perceived threat

↓

Arousal

↓

How you handle that arousal (what this book is all about)

↓    ↓

Anger    Rage

Notice that you can only feel anger when there is a reason to feel it. That reason is precipitated by an event, an interaction, a conversation, a relationship change, a workplace encounter, or other real or perceived interactions. That event is recognized by you, consciously or unconsciously, mentally or physically, as a threat to your sense of well-being. Both your mind and your body respond to that threat with an arousal designed to alert you and give you the energy to take care of yourself, to protect yourself in some way. Then, whether you are aware of it or not, you deal with the arousal you experience. The outcome of how you deal with arousal results in an organized and effective angry response or a disorganized, ineffective, or destructive rageful response. The goal of this book is to help you look at, understand, and change the way you handle arousal so that you can respond in an organized and effective manner when you feel threatened and aroused. In this book you will learn how to manage the physical and psychological arousal you experience and how to use physical and cognitive skills to more effectively respond to the original event. Again, that you will respond to the original event in one way or another is a given. Avoiding anger is one response. Exploding with rage is another. The goal of this book is to help you develop a healthy anger expression, which is the desired response.

## Understanding Anger

Simply put, anger leads to a constructive response to a threat. Rage leads to a destructive set of responses, and fear results in avoidance of conflict and threats. This basic differentiation provides the framework for understanding anger, which will help you understand and resolve conflict more effectively. When you are angry, you must integrate your emotional arousal with your thinking and purposeful actions to arrive at a constructive solution. This doesn't just happen. You have to learn this skill. Because anger most often occurs in relationships, the solution must work for both people in the relationship—that is, it must be bilateral. The problem is understood to be in the relationship, as is the solution. The following scenario illustrates how both people in a relationship are affected by the constructive handling of anger.

## ✦ Ned's Story

Ned's first response to his teenage daughter's rebellion was volcanic. When she said, "I hate you, you bastard! You never let me go anywhere! I'm going and you can't stop me!" he saw red. His own father had become enraged and physically violent when Ned was an out-of-control adolescent. Now what Ned felt well up in his body seemed like it was the rage that his father felt. He feared he was going to explode, verbally or physically. So Ned stepped back, took a deep breath, and said to himself, "She's not me and I'm not my father. I'm going to parent her in a healthy way." Then Ned stepped forward again and said in a firm, forceful, and steady voice, "You can be angry but you can't behave that way. Go to your room. You're grounded for the next hour. When you came out you can apologize. Then we can talk about what you're angry about without talking to me in that nasty and insulting manner." Ned's daughter looked surprised and was speechless. She started to stomp up the stairs, but was walking normally by the time she reached the top. Later she came down and talked with Ned about a recent fight with her boyfriend.

Ned initially experienced intense feelings when his daughter's behavior produced a problem for him. He recognized the strength and power of his feelings and his reaction to her. He could have simply acted out the intense energy he felt by yelling at her, shaming her, hitting her, or otherwise behaving in a destructive manner. But instead, Ned used his skills to calm and regulate his physical sensations without letting go of the problem. He resisted the pull toward a rageful response, recentered himself, and continued to parent his daughter in an appropriate way. Ned integrated his affective arousal with his goal of being a good parent and acted in anger, not rage.

Like Ned's behavior when he was parenting his daughter, anger can be strong and powerful but not destructive. Ned did not threaten her, or hurt her physically or psychologically. He acted in a powerful but constructive way. His goal was to solve the problem his daughter's behavior presented. He treated her in a constructive—not destructive—manner. Eventually she responded to Ned without the destructive behavior she had displayed earlier.

## Understanding Rage

Rage is a destructive approach to conflicts. Rageful responses do not integrate emotional arousal with thinking and purposeful action to constructively solve a problem. Instead, rageful responses are frequently very emotional, impulsive, and short-sighted, and they harm, humiliate, or destroy people, relationships, and trust. Rageful behaviors can be actively aggressive or passively or covertly destructive. In either case, they are destructive in their effect. Rageful behaviors silence, shame, intimidate, or otherwise eliminate the source of the threat. Rageful behaviors include

✦ physical violence

✦ shaming

✦ screaming

✦ intimidating

✦ controlling

✦ sarcasm

✦ silence

✦ refusing to talk about a problem

✦ sullen and sulking behaviors

✦ threats to end a relationship when attempts to control it don't work

✦ financial punishment

✦ verbal or emotional attacks

✦ humiliating a partner

✦ accusing and assigning malicious intent

✦ pathologizing or dehumanizing another

✦ punching a wall to intimidate or silence

✦ posturing as if you are going to hit someone, and verbal threats to hit if the other person doesn't comply

Notice that all these behaviors are destructive, or at least intimidating, which is destructive to relationships. A rageful person solves a problem, usually in a relationship, by destroying the source of the problem, that is, by hurting, shaming, or frightening the other person into submission. The intended effect of rageful behavior is to silence, control, or remove the problem. In a relationship, this is a one-sided, or unilateral, solution. The problem is still in the relationship, but the solution harms or limits the relationship, as the following example illustrates.

## ✦ Bill's Story

Bill had always felt threatened by his girlfriend. She was pretty, smart, and vivacious. She was more than he ever thought he deserved, and he knew he would never find anyone like her again. He was afraid she would see him for all his flaws and dump him for someone more attractive and confident. Over time, Bill's fear of his own inadequacy made him more and more jealous and possessive. One night, when Bill perceived his girlfriend to be flirting with a guy who was handsome and funny, he became enraged. By the time they got home, Bill was screaming at the top of his lungs. His girlfriend was frightened and kept saying she didn't do anything wrong. Bill's rage escalated. When she continued to argue and defend herself, Bill hit her. That solved the immediate problem. She was silent, and terrified. Bill solved the problem by frightening her into submission. Bill's behavior suggested that he could bully her into behaving the way he wanted. From now one, she would only pay attention to him. Bill's rage solved the problem in a one-sided and destructive manner. His girlfriend later broke off the relationship because she didn't feel safe, loved, or trusted.

Bill had felt threatened. His response, however, was clearly rageful and obviously harmed both his girlfriend and the relationship. Bill could have responded constructively, however. When he felt threatened, he could have expressed his anger by saying this: "You may not realize it, but it looks like you are flirting and coming on to other guys. Are you? If you are going to act that way, I don't want to continue this relationship. It doesn't work for me. You're still a good person and I value our time together, but we have different needs." Bill's girlfriend could then have responded in a variety of ways. She could tell Bill she wanted to continue the relationship, or she could have ended it. Bill's anger might have enlisted her help to solve a problem in the relationship.

# The Model

Understanding the real meanings and expected outcomes of anger and rage can lead you to better manage conflict and more effectively resolve problems. As noted earlier, anger and rage are both natural reactions to a perceived threat. But anger and rage do not come with names attached to them. You act on feelings based on what you've learned about what feelings are and what these feelings mean. If you learn new information about feelings and what they mean, you can behave in a way that is consistent with that new information. The following cognitive model is structured into five concepts that organize an understanding of anger, rage, and fear, and lead to a new set of skills you can develop to better express anger in constructive ways.

1. You can only feel anger or rage when you feel threatened in some way.

2. Anger is a constructive energy used to solve a problem created by the threat.

3. Rage is a destructive energy used to solve a problem created by the threat.

4. Fear is an energy to ensure your survival by limiting your responses to problems.

5. When people mistake anger for rage they either act violently or avoid conflict for fear of acting out. Anger avoiders will avoid conflict for fear of acting out of control.

## Concept One: Threats Trigger Anger or Rage

Your body is hardwired to ensure survival by alerting you to danger and providing you with energy to develop adaptive responses. Chapter 4 explores the physical and resulting behavioral arousal that is intended to ensure human survival. For now, it's important to note that your body has the same physiological response to a saber-toothed tiger as to an angry or untrustworthy spouse. Both present a threat to your sense of well-being. Both result in physical and psychological arousal, and ultimately, action. It is the perception of threat that activates a complex fight-or-flight response and triggers anger or rage.

### Understanding Threats

Threats challenge your sense of well-being. Threats can be universal: anyone would feel threatened when approached by three burly muggers. Threats can be uniquely individual: one person can find comfort in a completely dark room where another person feels terrified. Threats can be objective: a wife says to her husband in front of the whole family at Thanksgiving, "I'm leaving you." Threats can be subjective: a lover says, "I love you," yet seems to be very eager to leave early for his business trip to the city where his old girlfriend lives.

The perception of threat begins the anger/rage process of threat, arousal, and action.

### ✦ Ed and Tony

Ed and Tony were best friends, in spite of their differences. Ed was easygoing. He came from a loud, boisterous, friendly family. Kidding among his siblings was fun and funny. At family gatherings, Ed and his siblings would tell stories on each other. Some of the stories were embarrassing, but all was taken in good fun. When Ed's siblings told stories about the childhood antics and mistakes he made, Ed laughed and enjoyed them as much as anyone. He was not threatened by these stories. They did not provoke a sense of threat to him. In fact, he enjoyed the time spent together with his siblings.

Tony's family was more serious. Breaking the rules was uncomfortable and embarrassing. At family gatherings, when Tony's brother told stories about Tony's childhood behavior, Tony felt embarrassed. His face flushed and he broke into a mild sweat. When he tried to cut in on his brother's monologue, his brother would talk over Tony's objections. Tony felt exposed and shamed, even though the stories were not much different from those told about Ed. Tony would inevitably regret coming to a family gathering. He drove too fast going home and was short-tempered for days afterward. These two friends couldn't be more different. Ed enjoyed family events, whereas they threatened Tony and made him feel angry.

As noted above, threats can be from actual, objective events, or subjective or perceived events. An example of an objective event would be when you are yelled at unfairly by a coworker or you find the house a mess after your spouse promised to clean it. These events can be observed and witnessed. Threats can arise from subjective events as well. These would be events that are perceived as threats. For instance, you might feel embarrassed or slighted if your romantic partner shirked from holding your hand in public, or if it seemed your boss avoided eye contact with you.

### ✦ Alice and Patricia

Alice and Patricia were walking through the mall. There was a group of boys from their eighth grade math class in the mall. The boys spotted Alice and Patricia. Being awkward adolescents, the boys looked at the girls, kept talking among themselves, laughed, and walked away. Patricia was angry, thinking the boys were making fun of them. She said to Alice, "Look at them. They're laughing at us. I'm so mad, I'm not going to speak to any of them!" Alice responded, "Oh, don't bother with them. They're just awkward jerks. They'll grow out of it. They don't know how to come up and talk with us. My older brother did the same stuff when he was their age."

The boys may or may not have been laughing at the girls. Patricia reacted as if the subjective were objective, as if the boys really were laughing at them. Her reaction was based on her subjective experience. Alice's subjective experience allowed her to pass off the boys' behavior as evidence of their immaturity. She was not threatened by it.

## Anger Guards the Door to Real Feelings

The reason we feel threatened is rooted in the feelings masked by anger: sadness, hurt, or fear. These are the feelings and conflicts hidden by angry behavior. Sadness, hurt, or fear are tender and vulnerable feelings. We protect these tender feelings with our fierce feelings: anger and rage. It is when these tender and vulnerable feelings are activated that we feel threatened and perceive a threat to our sense of well-being.

This can happen on a variety of levels. Some interactions result in feeling fear on a physical basis, such as when someone threatens to hit you. Some interactions result in feeling hurt on an emotional or self-esteem basis, such as when someone makes fun of you in front of others. Interactions can make you feel sad on a spiritual level, such as when a loved one suffers an unfair physical ailment. Your tender and vulnerable feelings lie close to your sense of self. Anger and rage are the responses nature gives you to protect your sense of "self," so you cannot feel anger or rage without a threat to your sense of well-being. A threat to your sense of well-being in an interaction is associated with your tender and vulnerable feelings being activated. Anger protects these vulnerable feelings. You can only feel angry when you feel threatened.

### Feeling Powerless

Anger and rage are responses to a feeling of being out of control, and they seek to restore a sense of control. Human lives are characterized both by experiences of being in control and not being in control, of being powerful and being vulnerable, being fragile and being tough, being hurt and being resilient. No one is in control all the time, nor is anyone only fragile or vulnerable all the time. We experience both of these polarities. But one side of the polarity frightens us. We want to avoid feeling vulnerable, even though we are vulnerable, at least at some times and in some ways. We want to avoid feeling out of control, even though we are not in control of a lot of things that happen in our lives. We seek to protect ourselves from vulnerable feelings because they remind us of part of our experience as humans, that we are vulnerable to what happens to us, and cannot fully protect ourselves from death, injury, failures, and other human experiences.

Anger and rage serve the function of protecting us. In part, they represent the empowered part of the human experience. It is as if we are saying, "Yes, I might be powerless, but I can do something about it to protect myself; I am not entirely powerless." So we feel an energy that propels us to do something to protect ourselves. This is how anger is meant to be a messenger, a signal to alert us to a problem that threatens our sense of well-being. Anger and rage are always in relation to vulnerable feelings. They coexist. But we may only be aware of one of them at a time. Threats produce a sense of vulnerability, whether that sense is recognized consciously by us or not. Instinctively, we react with a fight-or-flight response via anger or rage, to protect ourselves. Threats are the key to understanding the triggering events that produce anger or rage.

## Varieties of Threats

Threats to your sense of well-being can arrive in a variety of forms. These include

✦ Physical threats—when a skateboarder nearly runs you down because he wasn't watching where he was going.

✦ Relational threats—when a partner or spouse flirts with someone else.

✦ Financial threats—when your spouse consistently outspends the budget and current bills can't be paid.

✦ Self-esteem threats—when what you consider your best work is held up for ridicule and an example of sloppy work.

✦ Spiritual threats—when you feel it doesn't pay to try hard; it seems the bad guy always wins.

✦ Professional threats—when a boss takes your work and claims it as his or her own, leaving you with nothing to show for your efforts.

✦ Parental threats—when your children disobey you and leave you feeling inept or incompetent.

✦ Lack-of-control threats—the intersection light turns red when you are already late for a business meeting.

✦ Social-desirability threats—when you overhear derogatory comments about your favorite features.

✦ Emotional threats—when you are ignored after asking for help in a meeting.

✦ Integrity threats—when you are unjustly accused of unethical conduct.

✦ Reputation threats—when an adversary spreads untrue rumors about you.

Any of these threats can provoke anger or rage. In each of the examples used in this book, the people described were motivated to protect themselves from more vulnerable feelings. Now you can see the level of threat posed by the interactions each of these people faced, and the tender and vulnerable feelings they were protecting themselves from.

Remember Ned and his teenage daughter? Ned's anger was triggered by his daughter's comments. He remained angry and dealt with her behavior in a parental and corrective manner. His anger was initially aroused by the same vulnerability his father had felt. Ned's daughter's behavior threatened his status as a parent and his competence as a father, and her name-calling hurt his feelings. He was vulnerable in that moment, and felt hurt, sad, and afraid. If his daughter's behavior did not provoke these feelings in him, he would not have felt the initial surge of anger. Ned's initial anger was fueled by the threat to his competence. His sense of well-being was threatened both by his daughter and by what the experience meant to him.

Bill hit his girlfriend because she flirted with another guy. Bill became enraged and destructive. Perhaps he could just as well have expressed his anger in a healthy manner, but, in any case, the reason he became aroused in the first place was that he felt vulnerable when she flirted with someone else. Bill's behavior served the purpose of protecting or masking his real and more vulnerable feelings, such as fear of rejection, humiliation, and loneliness. More than just self-esteem and social status was at stake for him; he feared he couldn't handle the experience at all. This was raw vulnerability, fear with a capital "F."

Bob avoided his anger. But the anger he avoided was actually triggered by the vulnerability he felt when his secretary performed poorly on the job. Bob was threatened by her behavior and feared his reputation and job security would suffer. Bob was in a position of authority, but he felt vulnerable and was deeply troubled by these feelings. He used avoidance to handle the situation.

Salinda avoided expressing anger over her husband's spending habits. She feared the financial disaster that lay ahead, and was hurt he didn't pay attention to her and the relationship and didn't keep track of their finances the way she did. She felt hurt, sad, and afraid, even when she avoided expressing her anger. She feared being seen as incompetent in her area of expertise.

Kathy hid her anger from herself and others. But she felt vulnerable and no longer had a sense of control over her own day. She felt sad and hurt that her father didn't pay attention to her as a person and saw her as a chauffeur. She was hurt and sad when her siblings offered no help and, instead, turned their backs on her. She was afraid for her own health and feared she would lose touch with friends who would grow tired of her unavailability to them.

Remember the original diagram of how people come to act in anger or in rage:

Event

↓

Perceived threat

↓

Arousal

↓

How you handle that arousal (what this book is all about)

↓↓

Anger    Rage

This section covered the first two parts of the diagram. It reviewed events that lead to a perception of a threat and what those threats are about. Anger is always related to other feelings that reflect the fact that people are vulnerable and can feel threatened. Threats trigger an arousal that leads to either angry or rageful, constructive or destructive, behavioral responses. The next section will focus on how anger can be constructive and what needs to happen to maintain a constructive outcome in the healthy expression of anger.

## Concept Two: Anger Is a Constructive Energy

In a healthy relationship, expression of anger is not threatening. Indeed, it can solve important problems and therefore strengthen the relationship. Healthy expression of anger also reinforces the relationship, for it communicates mutual respect. Each healthy expression of anger communicates three basic, unspoken assumptions about the relationship and the partner. The unspoken assumptions are

1. I respect you. I know you would not do anything to threaten or harm our relationship, or harm me in any way.

2. I respect myself. I know that I am reacting to something that is bothering me greatly, so it must be important.

3. I am bringing what is bothering me to you so we both can work on it. I can't fix it by myself. It is a problem between us and takes both of us to solve it.

These assumptions result from and generate trust. Healthy relationships can handle anger because it is not considered a threat, but rather a call to a partner to solve a problem so that closeness can be restored.

### Anger Is a Signal

Anger is a feeling that results from a threat, real or perceived, and results in some action, organized or disorganized, to respond to that threat. Anger signals us to protect ourselves. Anger is linked to a desire to fight back. For many of us, anger is a call to action. But to what kind of action?

Anger avoiders use anger as a signal to avoid taking action. Anger exploders use it as a signal to act violently. A constructive approach to anger allows you to see it as signal that a problem threatens your sense of well-being. While anger can alert you to a problem, it really doesn't tell you how to solve it. Instead, anger is like the messenger in the following story:

The commander of an outpost listens to a scout returning from observing the surrounding areas. The scout is quite agitated and excited, and says, "There's something going on out there, I'm not sure exactly what it is, but I know it may mean we are in danger!"

The commander can make several choices. Fearing conflict or escalation, he could dismiss the scout and act as if nothing had happened. Such behavior would not be wise or effective. In the anger model, the commander represents the anger avoider.

Alternatively, the commander could tell the excited and agitated messenger, who is not thinking clearly and is out of breath, wide-eyed, and alarmed, to get a bunch of troops and solve the problem himself. This would not be particularly wise or effective either. In this scenario, the agitated messenger is like an anger exploder who the commander would be turning loose.

Or the commander could thank the scout for his loyal service, and then decide upon a course of action to assess the situation and act in a manner to best solve the problem. In this case, the commander is wise and effective. He represents someone who expresses anger in a healthy way.

## Concept Three: Rage Is a Destructive Energy

Rage, as you have seen, is very different than anger. It is uncontrolled, irrational, and violent. Like anger, however, rage is a form of self-protection. If anger protects us by alerting us to solve a problem, rage protects us by destroying the source of the problem. Rage is destructive. Rage can have physical, verbal, or emotional expressions, and each expression is violent, furious, uncontrolled, and destructive.

These examples depict how rage is used to attempt to solve a problem.

### ✦ Ian's Story

Ian hit his son, hard. The blow stopped his son's threat to leave the house. It shut him up too. Ian didn't know what else to do. He had never been good at talking with his son. Now, with his son's adolescent energy, abruptness, testosterone, or whatever it was, Ian felt overwhelmed and out of control. He didn't know how to set limits or talk with his son. Yelling and screaming no longer worked. His son yelled and screamed as loudly as Ian. So he hit him, hard. That stopped him.

## ✦ Ann's Story

Ann felt hurt. She had seen her fiancé talking with another woman at the party. It was his office party, and she didn't know anyone. Ann felt insecure and shy, and wanted her fiancé to stay by her side. Later, on the way home, her hurt grew into feelings of betrayal and abandonment. The further away from the party she got, the more furious she became. Finally her fiancé asked, "What's wrong?" Ann wouldn't answer. He kept asking. He was getting more upset and worried, but she wouldn't talk with him. Finally he said, "You are hurting my feelings. I don't know what's wrong and you are not talking with me. This is really upsetting me." Ann just turned her face toward the car window, crossed her arms, and looked away. Finally she turned to him and said, "You are a typical, thoughtless, self-centered male. You can't think past your own nose, you idiot!" Ann was enraged. She communicated her feelings in a destructive way, and solved the problems of that evening at her fiancé's expense.

Ian's and Ann's behavior was destructive. Each felt threatened, but their responses did not solve a problem. Rather, each tried to win and shame or beat the other into submission. There was no basis of respect or safety in these expressions of rage. Each expression was dangerous, to the person or to the relationship.

Many anger avoiders did not grow up in families where anger was expressed. Most experienced the destructive expression of rage instead, but thought it was anger. By calling rage "anger," avoiders never learn to marshal their resources to solve a problem. They frequently confuse feelings, and end up feeling fear, which is neither anger nor rage.

## Concept Four: Fear Ensures Survival, but Limits Responses

Fear, or apprehension, is different from anger and rage. The expression "frozen in fear" captures this difference. While fear, like anger or rage, is a reaction to danger, fear, unlike them, is characterized by timidity, or a restriction of movement.

Fear protects us by ensuring our survival by withdrawing us from dangerous situations or withholding responses that could increase our exposure to, or perception of, danger or threat. Fear tends to constrain behaviors in response to a threat, whereas anger and rage propel people to act upon that threat. Fear and avoidance are understandable responses when you feel you don't have the resources or abilities to handle trouble or when you sense that trouble could hurt you, and trying to respond actively could only make it worse.

Anger avoiders experience fear as the basis of the drive to avoid anger. It may be rageful behaviors they fear, in themselves or in others, but the initial and dominating force is fear. Lois, depicted below, is fearful and has a limited response to her problem.

### ✦ Lois's Story

Lois was angry. Both of her teenage sons and her husband had left their clothes on the stairs and their dishes on the table. She felt as if she had three kids to clean up after. This was the third time this week that they had left a mess for her. She knew she was angry and was afraid that one of two things would happen: either she would get mad and yell at her family and then they would explode at her, or she would just go ballistic and then feel terrible about it. Instead of saying anything, Lois just quietly cleaned up the mess herself.

Lois feared she didn't have the resources to deal with the problem. She feared what she thought were the likely outcomes. When Lois avoided expressing her anger, it was actually rageful explosions she feared and avoided. Her fear constrained her responses to the problem. Lois functions as many anger avoiders do. She felt anger, then felt afraid of anger.

Lois's dilemma depicts the relationship between anger, rage, and fear. She initially felt anger, a natural response to a threat.

This threat was to her status as a wife and parent, and to her sense of well-being when the behavior of her loved ones made her feel like a servant instead of a wife and mother. Her anger was natural and normal. If she had acted with anger she would have told them how their behavior made her feel and she would have turned the chores over to them to do. But she confused constructive anger with destructive rage, feared her own feelings and responses, and avoided the conflict instead. Lois reacted as a classic anger avoider.

## Concept Five: Confusing Anger for Rage— Acting Violently or Avoiding Conflict

It's now possible to develop a different view of the internal experience of anger avoiders: anger avoiders confuse anger with rage, fear the effects of rage on themselves or others, and avoid anger as a result. Anger avoiders do this out of compassion and concern, not out of an intention to passively get back at the other person. They seek to avoid hurting others in the ways they have been hurt by "anger"—the rageful behaviors and personal hurt they have experienced or fear they will experience. Anger avoiders fear and avoid many normal experiences in relationships. Jerome is a good example of someone who fears anger and avoids conflict because he confuses anger for rage.

### ✦ Jerome's Story

Jerome came in for counseling with vague complaints. He described a lifelong tendency toward melancholy and chronically asked himself, "Why am I here? What am I supposed to do with my life?" He struggled with an addiction to cigarettes and missed the times in his life when he exercised regularly and felt better physically. Jerome said sleeping was always a problem for him. His inadequate sleep added to his general malaise. Jerome could "crank it up" and socialize well. In fact, at one job he was called "Smiley." But Jerome always felt the melancholy return whenever he was alone. He described his marriage as "stressed." Jerome said he and his wife had difficulty communicating and had no frank discussions anymore. They loved each other and had no major conflicts, yet there wasn't any positive energy either. Jerome's work was demanding, stressful, and started to take up more and more time. Jerome was particularly upset when he missed one week's regular Bible study class at church. He had to stay late at work when a coworker left early.

Clearly, Jerome was depressed. He had been on an antidepressant before without significant relief. Something else was needed. His therapist asked Jerome for more information about his marriage and his interactions at work. Jerome said that when he and his wife had disagreements, "We get quiet and back away." He added, "We're both sensitive. I try to be sensitive to her sensitivity. I don't want to be cruel or hurtful." Jerome said he and his wife take several days or longer before coming together and talking about their conflicts.

At work Jerome reported feeling overwhelmed. As a technician involved in complex medical equipment and procedures, it was very important that his work be done correctly. Jerome's coworkers did not share his commitment or diligence. Jerome said he would not confront his coworkers, but would follow up behind them instead, checking and correcting their work. This caused numerous interpersonal and administrative problems for Jerome. He felt isolated from his peers and unappreciated by his superiors.

Jerome internalized all this stress. The word "angry" was missing from Jerome's descriptions or reactions. He looked like, and acted like, a classic anger avoider: a real nice guy, competent and diligent at work, sensitive to his wife's emotional needs, looking for ways to be a better Christian, and keeping all his anger inside. Jerome's family of origin revealed what his anger avoidance was all about.

Jerome said he came from a good family. His parents never divorced and never fought, or at least never discussed any of their problems. His father was a heavy smoker and died of lung cancer four years ago. Jerome described his mother as someone who always put on a happy face, and tried to be optimistic and cover up her own troubles. She worked hard to convey a message that "all is well" and hid significant problems in her family and in her mood. Jerome's father's employment was erratic. They moved thirteen times as a result. They were living in Georgia when Jerome was sixteen and madly in love with a high school sweetheart. Jerome's father decided he wanted to return to New Jersey to be near his family. Jerome had always resented the constant moving and felt it was a major problem for him. But he never said anything until the move to New Jersey. Jerome was very angry and very adolescent. He told his father how he felt about this move and all the previous moves. He told his father how angry he was and that he wanted to stay where they were. Jerome described his father's reactions as if it had happened yesterday. Jerome's father sunk his head in his hands and cried. He looked decimated by Jerome's reaction.

Jerome said his father was always easily hurt. But this time Jerome felt he had injured his father with his outburst. Jerome also described other incidents where his father's response conveyed hurt and Jerome felt badly for how he made his father feel. But when asked bluntly, "Did your father ever get angry with you?" Jerome was taken aback. His father's anger, which could have resulted in normal parenting and limit setting, was something Jerome had never experienced or considered. Likewise, he could not recall his mother ever becoming angry at the constant trials presented by her siblings and parents. Jerome could acknowledge his resentment at his mother's false optimism and cheerfulness, and he noted that his melancholy was similar to hers when she wasn't putting on a happy face. But he never thought of her as angry.

From Jerome's stories about his family of origin it became clear that he learned to repress angry reactions because he was afraid of wounding others. He could not recall either of his parents ever expressing anger at him. Once Jerome realized that he had brought these patterns into his current life, he could begin to change for the better.

As he learned healthy anger expression skills, his depression lifted, he and his wife decided to address their troubles directly, and he worked on developing a relationship with a supervisor in which he could effect constructive change in the training, supervision, and evaluation process at work.

Like Bob, Salinda, Jerome, and many other competent, kind-hearted people you will meet in this book, anger avoiders assume that anger (a feeling of arousal) is the same as active destructiveness (a way of responding to that feeling). In fact, feelings and behavior aren't necessarily related at all. Simply put, feelings are our natural, unfiltered, unique response to events and interactions in our world. We are not necessarily responsible for what we feel. Our behaviors, on the other hand, are our deliberate, chosen reactions to events and interactions and we are fully responsible for them.

In this chapter you've learned why people suppress anger. In the next chapter you will see what happens when people suppress anger. Symptoms are always a good friend because symptoms tell us something is amiss. Without symptoms, anger avoiders would continue to avoid getting angry, and miss out on a lot of growth, trust, and safety.

# Changing Your Beliefs and Behaviors

Okay, pull out your journal. What did you learn in this chapter? Jot down any ideas that were new, or ideas that you previously had but had forgotten about. Make a list of the ideas generated by reading this chapter.

✦ What events threaten you?

✦ What is the nature of the threat that you experience?

✦ What are your assumptions about anger and rage?

✦ How have you labeled your feelings?

✦ What destructive or rageful responses have you used to deal with conflicts, threats, or problems?

✦ Do you use the same approach at home and at work?

✦ Are you more constructive in one setting and more destructive in the other?

✦ Do you convey respect when you are angry?

Look at your list. How do these ideas apply to the events, situations, and relationships in your life? What ideas can you put to use? How can you change your behavior in response to the threats that you experience?

Now try the three-step writing exercise I outlined in chapter

1. What happened in your life to make you feel afraid of anger?

2. How has that limited and affected you so far?

3. How are you going to think, feel, and behave now that you are regaining control of your own life again?

How did it feel to do this exercise at this point in your process of change? Hopeful? Challenging? Interesting? Keep going, there's more to do!

# 3

## symptoms of anger avoiders

Anger is an energy. As you will see in chapter 4, anger can be a very powerful energy. Before you even behave in an angry manner, you experience anger with your mind, with your feelings, and with your body. Anger brings distinct physical changes. Sometimes these physical changes can be strong, and experiencing these physical changes reveals the powerful energy you feel in your body when you are angry.

The word "emotion" has the word "motion" in it. In fact, as the author of *Boy Talk,* Mary Polce-Lynch (2002), points out, the Latin root of "emotion" is "to move." Anger is an emotion. It is meant to flow, both to you as a messenger, and through you, as an energy for protective action. When you stop that flow, symptoms occur. Anger builds up in your mind, in your feelings, and in your body. When you stop the flow of energy and bottle it up inside, it creates distress, or a state of dis-ease.

This chapter looks at what causes symptoms, what symptoms represent, and some of the predictable and observable results when we stop the flow of anger energy through us and keep it stuffed inside. To fully illustrate this as a human experience I will use full-length examples. The cases discussed here are reflective of the symptoms and dynamics anger avoiders experience on a daily basis, and are used to show what happens when energy is stifled and why symptoms occur.

# Going with the Flow

It is important that you flow with energy rather than stifle or stop the flow of energy. You were given the gift of anger, as described in chapter 2, to identify problems in your life in the form of threats to your sense of well-being. When you move with this energy, organize and utilize your resources, and figure out what needs to be done to most effectively solve problems, then they are resolved and you are alive with new growth and new opportunities. Relationships deepen with an earned and experienced trust. However, when you take energy, in this case anger, and turn it into fear and suppress it, a part of you is stagnant and dies (at least for the moment). You are then in unproductive distress and conflict. Symptoms are signs of unproductive distress and lack of movement.

# Symptoms Are Messengers

Symptoms are helpful because they tell you that something is wrong or amiss. Imagine what it would be like if you had no way to feel pain, physical or psychological. You might think that would be great. But if you had an infection and felt no pain, you might not know it was there, and you wouldn't seek treatment to heal it. The infection would fester and worsen until it became life threatening. Luckily, your body is wired to alert you to pay attention by sending you signals, in the form of symptoms, that there is a problem that threatens your health.

Psychological pain serves the same function. Psychological pain is manifested in the form of symptoms. In fact, there are very logical reasons why you would be in pain, or psychological distress, when you suppress anger and avoid handling conflict. When anger is suppressed, internal conflict results. This conflict will be expressed, one way or another. When anger is not expressed in its natural form, it will be expressed in a distorted form, such as symptoms of distress. There are three ways that suppressed anger, or any other strong feeling, will be manifested. But before getting into that, let's look at feelings and the energy they create.

# Feelings about Feelings

Feelings rarely create problems. But feelings *about* feelings almost always create problems. If you think about it, when you feel angry, you feel angry. When you feel sad, you're sad. That's all there is to it until you make something more out of that experience. Look at an infant or toddler. It is easy to tell when they are feeling angry, sad, afraid, or happy. They cry, laugh, and scream with abandon. As adults, we feel the same feelings. But instead of just feeling sad, we can feel embarrassed about feeling sad. Instead of simply feeling afraid, we can feel afraid of feeling afraid, fearing what others will think of us. Instead of simply feeling angry we can feel afraid of feeling angry or even angry about feeling angry. We have feelings about our feelings, labeling them good or bad. This creates problems.

Feelings are not good or bad. They simply are your unique reactions to events in your world. Your feelings are a basic way of expressing your individuality. After all, no one feels your feelings but you! Your feelings tell you about who you are and how you react to things. But when you have feelings about your feelings, you can develop additional conflicts. If you felt okay about feeling angry, or safe about feeling sad, you would not expect to experience troubles. But when you feel sad, ashamed, embarrassed, angry, or afraid of your feelings, you experience an inner conflict about being yourself. It is as if you say to yourself, "Are my feelings about the problem good or bad, right to have or wrong? Should I feel good about the way I feel or bad for having the feelings I have?" Anger avoiders, like many other people, feel deeply conflicted about having angry feelings. Anger avoiders not only have to deal with the energy represented in the first, natural feeling; they also have to deal with the feeling about the original feeling and the conflict that results. This dynamic creates an inner conflict that becomes a secondary problem, which results in symptoms.

# Anger Is an Energy

Basic laws of physics postulate that mass and energy cannot simply go away. At best, mass and energy can change shape, dimension, or form, but neither disappears. Anger is an energy. It has both physical and psychological properties, but it is an energy, nevertheless. If anger is suppressed, it must have some effect; it must go somewhere. Anger, like matter and energy, can change its shape, dimension, and form. These changes are distorted manifestations of the original energy and they take the form of symptoms.

## Working Double Duty

It takes energy to suppress energy. When anger is suppressed by applying even more energy to suppress it, a person has fewer resources, such as resiliency, tolerance, or determination, to handle other stressors and demands. If anger wells up and you push anger down, you have your energy moving up and being pushed down at the same time. That's exhausting! No wonder anger avoiders are frequently depressed and lack energy and motivation. They're exhausted.

To illustrate, take your left hand and put it under your right hand, left hand facing up and right hand facing down. Now push up with your left hand, but push down with your right hand. Make sure to push hard enough with each that you feel the strain and effort. Make sure your left hand doesn't win, but don't let it give up, even if it feels tired.

Your hands probably feel tense and are fighting against each other. The right hand has to exert more energy than the left, no matter how strong or driven the left hand is. Your left hand represents the normal, healthy arousal you feel when an event threatens your sense of well-being. You are aroused with physical and psychological energy to protect yourself. But your right hand represents the psychic energy you have to exert to repress either the arousal you feel or the expression of that arousal. You are literally working against yourself. The tension creates pain and discomfort, and it is exhausting!

After a few moments of this, your hands will be very tired. Doing normal housework may hurt more and be even more exhausting than usual. You will not have much energy in reserve. Because you are depleted, you will not be able to do your usual tasks, and you might be more short-tempered or easily bothered by things that would not usually bother you.

Welcome to the experience of chronically stuffing feelings! You can now understand the pain, stress, and discomfort that exist in your body when you avoid anger. This pain or stress is an energy and creates a secondary level of feelings or experiences that complicate the original feeling. When anger avoiders feel angry they have to use another feeling, such as fear, to suppress or push down the original anger. Feelings work against feelings, and energy is used against energy.

## Side Effects

In addition, instead of being discharged or manifested in change, growth, or resolution, stuffed feelings remain in stuffed and unresolved form. In the simplest terms, this feels bad and inhibits growth and development. Symptoms are a signal that something is amiss, psychologically or physically. Symptoms are usually not the problem, but rather an indicator of a real problem. Anger avoiders can experience psychological symptoms such as depression, psychological numbness (inability to feel anything), panic attacks, low self-esteem, fears, phobias, chronic feelings of alienation and shame, helplessness, hopelessness, and sometimes suicidal thoughts and feelings. As significant, painful, and awful as these symptoms are, they are not the problem but only indications of the existence of the real problem: avoiding anger, suppressing anger with fear (of destructive outcomes), and suppressing all of this into a stagnant energy that festers rather than flows.

Anger avoiders experience personal symptoms because of the energy they suppress or push down. Emotions, or feelings, are a psychological and physical energy, and must be either discharged (handled in a healthy way) or manifested somehow and somewhere in symptomatic form.

# Unhealthy Expressions of Feelings

In my experience there are three unhealthy avenues for expression when strong or persistent feelings are suppressed. There may be numerous healthy avenues for expression via creative problem solving; original expressions of art, poetry, or other artistic media; sublimation (turning negative feelings into positive actions); spiritual practices, such as giving yourself to a higher cause; healthy anger expression; or other more advanced ways to channel this energy into positive growth. After all, anger is an energy. Because it is an energy, it seeks expression. And because anger avoiders have feelings about feelings, such as fear of anger, symptoms are present. The conflict about expression of anger creates tension and pain, just like pushing one hand against the other, and symptoms occur as an expression of this inner conflict. If the original feeling were expressed in its original form, the secondary feelings and symptoms would never materialize. But when strong or persistent feelings exist and are not handled in healthy ways, most often they are expressed unconsciously or consciously as one of three kinds of symptoms:

1. psychological symptoms

2. behavioral symptoms

3. physical symptoms

## Psychological Symptoms

The first, psychological symptoms, are manifested in the subjective, or invisible internal world of the individual. Unlike physical or behavioral symptoms, psychological symptoms are more difficult to observe, measure, or quantify. Psychological symptoms are very real experiences to the individual experiencing them, but may be unnoticed by other people. Yet psychological symptoms have very powerful effects on everyone involved. Psychological symptoms range from chronic and predictable depression, low self-esteem, phobias, and anxiety, to more disturbing numbness and feelings of alienation, and other life-disrupting symptoms. In each case, most of the suffering occurs within the individual. Sometimes this suffering is unknown to others. But anger avoiders' relationships are impaired by omission (what does *not* occur, what is *not* done or said) more so than by commission (behavior that does occur). Their suffering affects everyone, directly or indirectly.

Here are three examples of the psychological symptoms manifested when anger is avoided and turned into fear. The first example shows the significant anxiety that occurs when conflict is avoided and left unresolved. Charlie's psychological symptoms were evident to him and everyone around him. His discomfort, as debilitating as it was to him, affected his wife as well. The second example involves more severe psychological symptoms, including a distorted sense of self and chronic overfunctioning. Kathy's psychological symptoms were very significant but were relatively invisible to others. She, however, was completely overwhelmed. The third example demonstrates the low self-esteem and chronic low-grade depression many anger avoiders experience. Joe's psychological symptoms were demonstrated in his chronic and long-term depression. He decided to avoid what he assumed was violence and screaming behaviors. He actually decided to avoid any and all conflict, no matter what the real outcome. But that decision hurt his marriage.

## ✦ Charlie's Story

Charlie's wife, Elaine, was as fiery as he was timid. They had worked out a comfortable arrangement. Charlie's income provided for the family and allowed Elaine to be a full-time mom. Charlie and Elaine loved each other very much and enjoyed the life they had together. But as time went on, the differences in their temperaments wore on each of them.

Elaine's father was a screamer. He frequently went on long tirades. No one ever told him, "Stop! Enough is enough!" So when he got started on something, he went on and on, just as Elaine did. It wasn't that Elaine intended to hurt and shame Charlie. But she did, nevertheless. When she was angry, she'd "go off" and yell or scream at Charlie. It seemed to Charlie that it went on forever. It never occurred to Elaine to make her point clear once and then stop. She repeated and repeated herself and went through lengthy litanies of past offenses. She talked constantly when she was angry.

Charlie's family never talked about anything. Charlie's mother died when he was eight, and his father remarried two years later. No one ever talked about how his mother died. Charlie's father glossed over it and avoided telling Charlie what had happened. Charlie was too young and too insecure and lost to ask what had happened to his mother. In fact, Charlie didn't find out the real story until he was thirty-seven years old. Furthermore, there was a rift between his biological mother's family and Charlie's father just after her death. All of a sudden, Charlie didn't see or play with his cousins anymore. No one said why. He wondered why he no longer played with them. Charlie never found out the reasons for the rift as a child. He didn't even ask why until he was well into his adult years.

Charlie and Elaine were an odd but perfect match. She had never learned to contain, control, or direct her long verbal tirades. Charlie had never learned to stand up for himself, question or confront anyone about anything, or ask for what he wanted. As the years went on, Charlie became more and more timid at home. Elaine continued to go on and on with her verbal tirades. As Charlie became more timid, Elaine became more verbose. They still loved each other and were fully committed to the marriage, but affection gradually waned and frustration grew in each of them. Elaine expressed her frustration in her tirades. Charlie's timidity turned into avoidance and discomfort, which grew into a chronic anxiety. Charlie was uncomfortable with Elaine's tirades. He wanted to tell her to stop but became more and more anxious, depressed, frightened, and withdrawn instead.

Once again, Charlie felt alone and lonely, just as he had after his mother died. He felt no more able to stand up for himself and his needs now than he had felt then. Yet he still needed comfort and connection. Charlie became more overtly anxious and deferential. That's when he began to enter chat rooms on the Internet and find people who seemed to understand and care. Even though they were anonymous, or perhaps because they were anonymous, Charlie felt understood and appreciated. He developed what seemed like real feelings and real connections to these faceless people with whom he could communicate and share his feelings and needs. Elaine eventually found out. She felt betrayed and outraged, and threatened to end the marriage. Charlie felt as if his world were falling apart.

When Charlie came to therapy, he looked ill. He shook all over and stammered through his words. All he could do was repeat both in therapy and at home, "I'm sorry, I'm sorry. I promise I'll never do it again." Charlie could barely function at work and needed medication to sleep. Elaine was just as committed to the marriage as before, but her anger was totally unleashed, even more so.

Charlie was angry at Elaine's tirades, but he felt fearful and anxious instead. He had no real way to recognize his own anger, talk about his needs in a real relationship, say "Stop!" to Elaine, or otherwise create a better solution to her tirades.

Elaine was an anger exploder. Charlie was an anger avoider. Each had new skills to learn. Elaine eventually learned to connect with Charlie before she expressed her anger. She would tell him she had to talk with him and ask if it was a good time. She was careful to express her appreciation for him before saying what bothered her. She learned to name a problem and ask Charlie to solve it with her, trusting that it was his intention to improve the relationship. Charlie, in turn, learned to manage his fear by taking a deep breath and talking to himself to focus and direct himself. He would say, "She's angry but she's not going to hurt me. I can handle this, listen to her, and work through the problem. I don't have to give in to fear." Gradually they both learned new skills, developed a real relationship based on the solutions they forged together, and developed a deep trust in place of the habit and assumptions that once ruled.

## ✦ Kathy's Story

Remember Kathy from chapter 1? Kathy feared anger could only mean violence. And violence, even the most vague threat of violence, frightened her. She saw the potential for violence in any conflict or even in mild disagreements. She showed up for her first therapy session debilitated by anxiety. She called her husband once or twice a day for reassurance and comfort, greatly interfering with his work. Kathy could not complete many basic chores at home, such as cleaning the dishes or vacuuming and dusting the rooms. Kathy felt overwhelmed by anything and everything. She drove her father everywhere he wanted to go and listened to her sister's accusations of Kathy being selfish when Kathy asked her sister to help. Kathy rearranged the family finances to pay for her adult nephew's expenses when he stayed with them and ran up Internet and phone charges. Kathy had a lot to be angry about, but all of her anger seemed to have turned into anxiety.

Kathy spent her day taking care of everyone's needs. It had always been that way. Kathy was the youngest of three. She was seven years younger than her brother and nine years behind her sister. Her parents were violent alcoholics. Kathy saw her drunken father fly into rages and beat up her brother regularly. Her mother seemed to hate her sister and frequently beat and shamed her, yelling obscenities and accusations. Kathy was spared the beatings. Perhaps her parents were older and tired. Or perhaps the alcohol had taken a toll on their physical abilities. For whatever reason, Kathy did not receive the horrific beatings she witnessed. She wasn't spared the shaming, however, and that felt just as injurious to Kathy as the beatings she watched. Kathy's mother frequently said, "How dare you tell me, 'No.' You should be ashamed of yourself," when Kathy was playing with dolls and didn't want to do her siblings' chores. Her father was intolerant. He told Kathy she would never amount to anything. No one took Kathy's side, protected her, or stood up for her. Extended family members took a hands-off approach to the entire situation.

Kathy grew up alone and overwhelmed. Her brother fought back and carried the psychological and physical scars to prove it. Her sister tried to fight back, but her mother never let up. Without knowing that she knew it, Kathy understood that her anger was a liability. It could only make the situation worse. If she expressed anger or displeasure at her parents, she feared they would unleash all their violent and destructive forces on her. She was a little girl, alone with her anger in a hostile world. In a manner of speaking, Kathy became her own worst enemy. She learned early on to completely suppress her anger and be meek, timid, and fearful instead. These feelings kept her safer than expressing her anger could. Kathy feared even the thought of resisting or disobeying her parents. Eventually she became afraid of resisting anyone about almost anything. Kathy forgot the original anger she felt. After all, it was only a liability. Instead she experienced her anxiety and grew to know herself as an anxious person.

Like many children in abusive homes, Kathy had come to hold the belief that if she could somehow be a better girl the abuse would stop. Children are naturally egocentric. They believe that abusive events are their fault. Children confuse feeling bad, a natural feeling when watching a parent hit an older sibling, with being bad.

Kathy felt bad when she either witnessed or received any abuse, physical or psychological. This happened so often in Kathy's family that she felt bad all the time.

No matter what Kathy did, the violence continued. Kathy feared that this was because she was bad. She tried to help her family by being good. Being good meant being helpful, studious, pleasant, and cooperative. Being angry meant being bad.

As an adult, Kathy was limited by the coping style she had developed as a child. Kathy thought she was afraid of anger, but what she actually feared was the destructive expression of anger—rage. Kathy had never experienced anger and looked befuddled when her therapist described healthy anger expressions. Kathy didn't know anything about anger or healthy conflict. She grew up with rage and lacked the skills to organize, understand, or express healthy anger. When Kathy felt the physiological symptoms of anger, such as rapid heartbeats, flushed skin, or rapid breathing, she thought the only possible outcome was that she would behave the way her parents did.

Long ago, Kathy had vowed to never "be angry." Actually what she meant to vow was to never be hurtful and destructive to other people. Since she knew nothing about healthy expressions of anger, Kathy naturally assumed, consciously and unconsciously, that she could either be a good girl and cooperate or be a bad girl and be mean, vengeful, and destructive. Kathy could understand the concepts of anger and rage, and understood how she had developed such a fear of expressing her anger, but initially, she could not apply these ideas to herself and change her way of dealing with the stressors in her life. She felt she would be a bad person if she resisted anyone about anything. So her therapist talked with Kathy about expressing healthy anger as a way to establish a sense of self separate from the good girl and bad girl images that had limited her.

Healthy anger never existed in Kathy's family. Physical rage, not anger, was the norm. Emotional rage was expressed in the shaming, accusations, and name-calling that took place. When Kathy couldn't complete her own activities, homework, or reading, without suddenly being called to take care of her mother's demands, her own anger wasn't tolerated. So when Kathy was describing her daily schedule and the intrusive calls from her father to be driven to his latest whim, her therapist asked, "What would happen if you said, 'I know you don't intend to make my day unmanageable, but you do. I need you to respect the life I have with my family and not assume I can take care of you all the time. I'm sorry but I have other plans today.'" Kathy stopped short, looked at her therapist in dismay, and even seemed to stop breathing. Her therapist continued. "After all, Kathy, you are angry. Your body knows it: you feel aches and pains all over, and you don't sleep well. Your mind knows it: you feel depressed and have chronic panic attacks. The little girl in you, the 'old you' tries to solve problems by being a good girl and complying with any and all expectations placed upon you. But the 'new you' can learn that facing conflict, even saying no, doesn't mean you will hurt your family, it doesn't mean that they will behave the way they used to, and, if they do, it doesn't mean you are still a little girl and will be permanently injured by them anymore. You can be angry and say no without being mean."

Over time, Kathy explored her old assumptions about violence and destructiveness and found ways to develop new ideas and skills about healthy expression of anger. From there Kathy was better able to develop her own style of conflict and healthy anger expression because it further differentiated the new "me" from the old "not me," or her way of being angry from her family's way of raging.

### ✦ Joe's Story

Joe's wife dragged him into couples counseling. He wasn't kicking and screaming, as many men do. In fact, he was quiet and attentive. Joe cooked, cleaned, and supervised bedtime routines. He wasn't particularly interested in watching sports on TV and didn't go out for long Friday nights with the guys. In many ways he was the ideal husband. But Joe was lifeless. He knew it. Joe considered himself a plugger, someone who simply plugs through one day and on to the next, getting necessary work done but not enjoying life. He went to work, did his job, and came home and did his job. Joe didn't have fun or ever enjoy himself. Worse yet, he didn't think he deserved more. After all, his life was so much better than what he had experienced as a child.

Joe's family story was similar to many. He had one out-of-control parent and one seemingly absent parent. His father was in a world of his own. Joe could remember looking out the living room window of the house, seeing his father sitting in a lawn chair sunning himself or reading. Joe's father seemed oblivious to the chaos in the family, and never helped his wife or protected his kids from her wrath. Joe's mother, in the meantime, was a constant cauldron of conflict and turmoil. She was angry all the time. She was a relentless tyrant. She seemed to hate joy, playfulness, or spontaneity, and immediately squashed any sign of these traits in her children. It was dangerous to be alive in Joe's house. Anything that moved unleashed her unbridled and destructive rage. Her mood fell in torrents on all the children. Any behavior, any interaction, any movement on the part of her three children unleashed a barrage of criticism, blaming, and accusations. Pretty soon Joe learned how to become invisible. He killed his own spirit and successfully suppressed laughter, joy, play, conflict with his siblings, or anything else that would incur his mother's wrath. And like Kathy, in the previous story, Joe's appropriate childhood solution significantly limited his adult life.

Joe avoided all conflict. He assumed conflict meant violence and screaming. Joe didn't argue with Nancy about the things he didn't like; he simply and quietly complied. When her way of keeping the house or parenting the kids differed from what he thought was reasonable, he did it her way nevertheless. Joe successfully avoided screaming matches and a lot of bad feelings, but he also avoided a lot of good stuff too. He knew the old adage that a couple has to fight well to love well. He heard the phrase about not taking anger to bed at the end of the day. Joe negotiated these quandaries by simply not being angry in the first place. But when he avoided anger, he also avoided intensity, the trust that comes from successful conflict resolution, and the enjoyment of family life. He knew he was missing a lot. That's why he felt so poorly about himself. He just didn't want to risk it all and bring in the anger that ruined his childhood. Joe didn't want to cause any trouble.

Joe exhibited what is called a chronic low-grade depression. He could function adequately, did not miss work, and did not exhibit any overt symptoms such as excessive drinking, numerous medical or health problems, or any violent or obviously destructive behaviors. Joe could easily discuss his low self-esteem. He just didn't think much of himself. In fact, he simply didn't like himself. The idea that anyone would like themselves made him laugh. Joe defended his mood and lifestyle, saying it was "each generation's job to advance the ball ten yards." Eventually some future generation will get it right and score some kind of emotional or familial touchdown and be happy. Joe saw it was his job to advance ten yards from the family he grew up in. That ten yards meant stopping the violent and shaming outbursts. It did not include having much fun or enjoying himself.

Joe's wife, Nancy, complained that she didn't get anything from him. He listened to her but did not tell her how he felt about her. Joe loved his wife and admired the thoughtfulness she brought to the family, the way she could be gentle and firm with the kids, and how she brought the same spirit to her work as a teacher. Joe told friends about his wife and what he thought of her. Joe never told Nancy, fearing that would spark emotions in his marriage and bring joy to his life. Joe wasn't prepared for that.

Joe was initially resistant to changing his behavior or his belief that he didn't need to change. He was content with his "ten yard gain." But when Nancy became more unhappy and expressed anger and disappointment at his flat mood and lifeless attitude, Joe's world began to change. He felt an old familiar discomfort. Nancy's behavior reminded him of how he felt when his mother was critical. Nancy was not his mother, but Joe remembered how he felt back then, and felt the same feelings now. He still didn't have a way to deal with Nancy's anger or his own, which was beginning to creep into his interactions with the kids. The collapse came when Joe screamed at his oldest son over a minor incident. The ten yard gain theory didn't work anymore. Joe now had to come to terms with his real feelings about his family of origin and develop new skills to live with Nancy and the kids.

In time, Joe remembered the fear and terror he felt when his mother attacked everyone. He also remembered his anger at her behavior as well as at his father's. Reconnecting with his angry feelings led him to take charge of his anger and break the family pattern of exploding or avoiding. Eventually he became a better husband to Nancy and a more fun loving father to his kids.

In all three examples, these adults suffered primarily psychological symptoms. They experienced depression, anxiety, a sense of helplessness, and relationship limitations. In each case the primary problem was what they did not do, rather than what they did do. Most often, anger avoiders experience psychological symptoms and suffer more than they appear to suffer. They use more energy to push down the anger that wells up in them. As a result they feel exhausted, overwhelmed, and inadequate. As a result they tend to withdraw or suppress even more, creating a vicious cycle. Each of these people was able to face inner conflict by revisiting its origins and find better resolutions to adult problems than the patterns formed in childhood.

## Behavioral Symptoms

Anger avoiders experience behavioral problems as well. Not all symptoms occur within, or inside, an anger avoider. It is not realistic to think that your behavior would be disconnected from your feelings. Certainly in children, this difference is immediately evident. If you want to know how a child feels, look at his or her behavior. Behavior is a language of expression, for children and adults. Happy children laugh, play, share, recover from disappointment or mistakes, and develop tolerance or understanding for the mistakes of others. Unhappy children scowl, fight, get hurt easily, and don't recover from their own mistakes or the mistakes of other kids.

Not only is it easy to tell how children feel from observing their behavior, you can also predict children's behavior based on their experiences. If a child is nurtured, taught, loved, believed in, and feels understood, that child will behave in a predictable way. If another child is constantly punished, accused of wrongdoings, real or imagined, and criticized for every misstep, that child will also behave in a predictable manner. The first child will be more likely to play fair, share, work now for rewards or gratification later, and smile or laugh a lot. The second child may be more likely to get into fights, try to win at all costs, get behind in homework or school tasks, and cry or scowl more often. Each child would "speak a language" through their behavior, and that behavior would reflect their inner feelings and experiences. Their feelings would be expressed through and have a direct influence on their behavior.

Adults aren't really any different. You can usually tell when someone you know is having a bad day. They act troubled, grumpy, distant, preoccupied, or inattentive. You may notice some other observable change in their behavior, but you can see that their behavior is affected by their feelings. As discussed earlier, anger avoiders have feelings about their feelings and end up feeling troubled about being themselves. This creates a state of dis-ease. There is an inner experience of this dis-ease, through psychological symptoms. There is also an outward expression of dis-ease through distorted behavior. The ways behavior can be influenced are as varied as the characteristics people manifest.

Anger avoiders and anger exploders are directly related. Anger avoiders fear that the only expression of anger is an explosion. That is the only expression they know. When they cannot avoid their anger anymore, for whatever reason, they explode. So, frequently, anger avoiders explode, then feel guilty, fear anger even more, and return to a full avoidance of anger. Anger avoiders and exploders share the same common misconceptions talked about in chapter 1. Despite the outward differences, anger avoiders and anger exploders are more similar than different.

### ✦ Jimmy's Story

On first glance, Jimmy seemed as easygoing as a guy could be. He laughed and smiled at anything. His face was always breaking into a grin. Yet he had learned the art of hiding his real feelings from everyone, especially himself. Jimmy and his wife came in for couples counseling because sometimes he would fly into rages. He slammed doors, screamed, threatened to leave, and cussed up a blue streak. His wife, Mary, was frightened during these outbursts. Jimmy would scoff at her fear, saying, "I've never hit you and never will!" Jimmy could not feel empathy for her. He was too lost in his own fear, but he didn't recognize his own fear. Jimmy's rages brought a crisis when his wife decided not to be afraid anymore and took a stand. Either they get help or she was "out of there."

Jimmy had a horrific story to tell. He was beaten or abandoned almost daily throughout his childhood. He described his family as mean-spirited, and without limits in their expression of any irritation. Jimmy's story was even more outrageous than most, and made more so by his facade of smiles. His wife knew nothing about his childhood. She married the nice, easygoing guy she met. The rageful Jimmy appeared as soon as the marital glow faded and the usual couple problems emerged. Jimmy was as verbally violent as his family was physically violent. He knew no limits. Yet all the fights were unproductive, and Jimmy was driving his wife out the door. He loved her so much he couldn't see living without her, so he came in for counseling willing to change but defended.

Like many men, Jimmy had never told his story to anyone. Jimmy had some sense that his childhood was different than most, but because he had never told the whole story, the magnitude of the abuse was masked even to himself. Jimmy learned only one response to conflict: all-out war. He didn't want to continue the family legacy, but he knew no recourse. Yelling was in every cell in his body. It was all he ever knew.

Jimmy avoided and avoided. But when he couldn't avoid anymore, he exploded. When he was angry over the usual stuff that comes up in marriages, Jimmy's body reacted before he could ever organize his thinking. He yelled instinctively. Not because that's what he actually wanted to do, but because that's what he knew to do. As conflict increased, so did Jimmy's explosions. Jimmy wanted to learn how to behave and handle his anger in a different way. He simply had no idea what that way could be.

Gradually, as Jimmy told his story, two things changed. First, his wife began to understand his behavior. She became less frightened as she saw that Jimmy was committed to ending the violence he grew up in. Second, Jimmy began to understand himself. As he told his story and "got it outside" himself, he could hear it from an objective perspective, compare his story to other families, and reevaluate his experiences in childhood. He began to have empathy for himself and for the experience his wife encountered with him. As he learned healthy anger expression, he was able to stop his verbal violence.

## ✦ Frank's Story

Frank survived what he considered his worst nightmare, a personal relationship that ended up in a public disaster. He had found a beautiful woman who enjoyed the same things he liked: travel, entertainment, literature, and a desire to see the world. They dated for a while. Frank had been a bachelor for quite some time and owned his own house. When she asked about moving in with him, he bristled but did not share his real thoughts. She moved in, and the result was disastrous.

Frank had always been an easygoing guy. He made his living on his sociable temperament, and never had confrontations with people. Frank could sell flea powder to fleas and leave everyone with a smile on their faces. He wasn't manipulative, just pleasant. Frank liked it that way. Ever since he was a kid, he was that way.

Frank grew up in a good family. They were well behaved and accomplished. Both of his parents were supportive of all the kids. But Frank grew up with mild learning problems. Frank knew he was different, and all the nurturing in the world did not erase the academic struggles he faced. He got through school but did not earn degrees or gain academic standing, like the rest of his family did. He got through because he had to. Frank felt inferior in his family and in school. But he was good, really good, at being a nice guy. He felt good about himself when he was able to get people to smile and feel comfortable with him. After school, Frank became a salesman. He was good at it because he pleased people and never put his ego first. He listened well, learned what people needed, and sold it to them. Life had become comfortable for Frank. He had lots of friends, traveled, and loved to entertain.

When his girlfriend asked about moving in with him, Frank was unprepared to say no. It had never been his style. He didn't want her to move in now. Maybe later, maybe not. Frank liked being a bachelor. But she did move in. And Frank began a downhill spiral. He still was easygoing and pleasant, but secretly he felt grouchy and unhappy. When his girlfriend would ask a favor from him, he would become more resentful.

The relationship quickly soured. His girlfriend had given up the lease on her place and was stuck where she was, at least for now. Things became more tense. She didn't know what was wrong, and Frank never told her directly. Instead he stayed away from home more. Frank felt more and more uncomfortable. His girlfriend was angry at Frank's behavior and felt more betrayed and resentful. She argued with him about things that they hadn't argued about before.

One day, Frank told her to get her own place. This made her more angry. She said defiantly, "No." Frank was flustered. When she tried to call a friend, Frank became frightened that she might say something unpleasant about him, and he abruptly grabbed the phone out of her hand. His girlfriend was now physically frightened. She went to another phone and called the police. Now Frank faced a domestic violence charge.

Ironically, Frank was the most gentle and easygoing person you could meet. No one would believe Frank could be violent. Frank told no one. He was so ashamed he hid the information from everyone.

Frank was a classic anger avoider in many ways. His easygoing nature became his only style of interacting or handling conflict. He became very skilled at being easygoing, but was equally unskilled with direct confrontation and conflict. When conflict became unavoidable, he reacted impulsively. He felt threatened and reacted out of a fight-or-flight response. But the abruptness of his actions made him come across as an anger exploder. He frightened his girlfriend when in fact he was the one who was frightened.

## ✦ Derek's Story

Unfortunately, Derek was very talented. He could fix anything, and probably had repaired just about everything. He was known as a nice guy, someone you could turn to when you needed help. A huge man, he was as big and strong as he was gentle and kindhearted. The trouble was that Derek was never home. He was always working to support his family, or he was fixing something that a friend or acquaintance asked him to fix. Sometimes these people asked him to lend them money to get out of a tight place. Derek would fix that problem too.

His wife was angry, lonely, and fed up with the constant requests that Derek felt obligated to fill. Derek couldn't say no. He would offer excuses such as, "I just like helping people," or "It feels mean to say no when I know I can do it," or "I don't want to see anyone hurting when I could help." Derek worked his regular job, from 7 A.M. to 4 P.M., and then ran his own business three or four nights a week. He responded to requests for help after that, and it wasn't unusual for him to get home after 1 or 2 A.M. Then he would get up with four hours of sleep and tackle another day.

Derek's wife was about to leave. He didn't want her to go, but he didn't want to face the discomfort of telling people he couldn't do what they asked of him.

Derek's family history was unremarkable. His father worked a lot, but not to the degree that Derek did. His mother raised Derek, his two brothers, and two sisters. As children, they were expected to obey their mother's directives. It seemed to Derek that his childhood was not unusual and that everyone got along okay. There was no significant pattern of abuse, shaming, or other predictors of anger avoidance. Derek somehow had turned being a nice guy into a full-time job, with no time off for good behavior. No matter how much he did yesterday, he still was available today for whatever the need happened to be. Derek couldn't, or better said, wouldn't change his behavior. Derek was avoiding conflict, either real conflict with his wife or conflict he imagines he would have with friends if he were to say no. He became mildly upset with his wife because of her constant complaints. He became more upset when she started getting a babysitter and going out without him. He pleaded with her to stay home. But he was never home, and in the end she asked him to leave.

Derek did not come from a family with classic anger avoider patterns. Perhaps he learned to be gentle because he was so big. Perhaps it was from peer or cultural influences to stay in control, or from his attempts to compensate for fears and inadequacies. Whatever the origin, Derek could see no other way to be himself than to be a constant help to anyone around him. He imagined conflict where it wasn't, and anticipated people being hurt if he said no, even when they didn't feel hurt. Derek's perception of himself was so limited he couldn't tolerate the challenges brought on by change.

Derek was completely out of touch with his own feelings, needs, and desires. As is the case with many anger avoiders, Derek lost himself through avoiding conflict and trying to take care of everyone else. He tried to make everything okay for everyone. But he couldn't. The further he went with this pattern of behavior, the more he faced the uncomfortable conflict he had so carefully avoided.

Jimmy's, Frank's, and Derek's behaviors revealed their symptoms, or the effects of avoiding conflict and expressions of anger. It is not unusual for men to display inner conflict through unhealthy behavior patterns. (Chapter 9 will show you why this is the case.) Some anger avoiders, like Jimmy, grew up with violence and destructive behavior and vowed not to repeat the same. Some, like Frank, simply lack skills, experience, or exposure to healthy expression of anger and act impulsively when they reach the end of their current coping style. Some, like Derek, lose themselves in being a "nice person" and never develop a sense of their own direction in life.

## Physical Symptoms

The third symptomatic avenue when strong or persistent feelings are suppressed is physical. These symptoms are real, painful, life changing, and can lead to life-threatening conditions. The mind and body are one. When you feel anger, fear, panic, or joy, your body changes to reflect that feeling state. It is not possible, for instance, for your heart to be racing, your skin to flush, your muscles to tense and become rigid, and your breathing to be rapid and shallow while in your mind you feel peaceful and serene. Similarly, it is not possible to think intensely and become absorbed in thinking about something that has completely enraged, humiliated, or frightened you and have your body remain completely at rest and in peace. Clearly, your mind and body join together to provide you with emotional and physical experiences that are integrated. Otherwise your feelings or experiences would not feel fully real. As you will see in chapter 4, the mind and body are intricately linked, and you feel emotions with your body even more than you do with your mind.

As your emotions are in your body, so is the stress of suppressing emotions. These repressed emotions are manifested in your body as physical distress.

Anger avoiders can and do experience physical distress as manifestations of the blocked flow of energy. Keeping that much emotional energy locked up in the body over a long period of time has enormous consequences for health and well-being.

Here are two examples of symptoms of anger avoidance that are expressed physically. Nancy's desire to be a "better person" blocked her awareness of her own anger. But her body remembered and recorded each incident. Nancy had to learn to recognize the language of her body and translate symptoms back into their original triggering events before she could develop better anger responses. Willie, too, was a very nice person. He never expressed or revealed his anger, but his body did.

## ✦ Nancy's Story

Nancy grew up with violent, alcoholic, chaotic parents. She tells the story of when her father was in an alcoholic rage one night and her mother took the rest of the family to spend the night at Nancy's grandmother's house. When they returned in the morning, Nancy saw broken lamps and doors and a knife stuck in the wall above the kitchen door. Nancy told numerous stories about her father's "anger" and the abusive, destructive consequences. She suffered physically and emotionally, from beatings and being shamed by her father's name-calling and accusations. Nancy always tried, as do most abused children, to be a better girl so her father wouldn't be so angry all the time. She thought, both consciously and unconsciously, that if she only were a better girl that he would stop being "angry." Nancy committed herself to being that good girl. She excelled in school, graduated from college, and landed a very responsible job in a helping profession. By all appearances, Nancy had it made: a great job, a steady marriage, two healthy kids, and a promising future at work.

But Nancy was in constant physical pain. She took pain medication, had endured a variety of medical procedures designed to alleviate her pain, and missed family functions and occasionally work days because of it. Nancy had seen medical and mental health providers specializing in pain management, but had gotten no relief. On a scale of one to ten, with ten being unbearable pain, Nancy rated her constant state as "an eight, maybe eight and a half." Nancy was referred to a therapist when her pain management specialist retired.

She talked to the therapist in more depth about her relationship with her husband and her supervisor. Her husband was a traditional male and expected Nancy to be a traditional female. He considered himself to be the man of the house, best equipped to make decisions or handle problems. He frequently told her what to do to handle situations at work, interrupted her parenting with the kids, and shielded her from financial bills and other issues.

As she talked to her therapist, Nancy was able to see that these interactions with her husband often caused her physical pain. Just talking about certain incidents made her pain level increase.

She talked about one incident in which she had left the room after her husband had told her that he could handle a situation with the kids better than she was handling it. Upon leaving the room, she had felt a lot of pain. Her therapist asked, "If you hadn't been feeling pain at that moment, what would you have felt instead?" Nancy immediately shot up in her chair. "I was angry!" she blurted out. Nancy had learned from earlier talks that she chronically suppressed anger and compensated by trying to be perfect.

Nancy also rated her level of pain during her conversation with her therapist. After initially talking about the incident, she rated her pain as an eight on a scale of one to ten. After she blurted out that she was angry, she rated her pain as a six on the same scale. Her therapist then asked Nancy what she might do with the anger that she felt. Nancy looked defeated. She said, "I wouldn't do anything." Her pain level was back up to an eight.

Nancy was beginning to feel and own her anger, but lacking the skills or an understanding about a constructive outcome, she relapsed back into avoiding anger. Nancy's case reflects the diffi-culties experienced when symptoms are manifested in physical distress. These patterns do not seem to change as quickly as is the case with psychological or behavioral symptoms. Nancy was deeply conflicted about her own feelings, and had suppressed them for so long that she had a very difficult time learning to both recognize her feelings and change her behavior. In time, Nancy learned, in spite of her fear, and with an awareness of her pain, to take risks and change her approach to conflict. She needed a very structured approach (similar to the one that will be described in chapter 4). With repeated efforts and occasional relapses, Nancy learned to organize her resources and manage conflict more constructively.

### ✦ Willie's Story

Willie was quiet, gentle, and lonely. He longed for a meaningful relationship and began counseling to find out why he was not able to start and maintain one. Willie often spoke with a mild stutter, and his skin broke out in rashes very easily.

Willie never told anyone when he was angry. Clearly his feelings were frequently hurt, yet no one knew. When he felt hurt, Willie would quietly, almost imperceptibly, back away from the relationship, leaving the other person wondering where he went. Willie would then retreat into a familiar world of hurt, disappointment, and loneliness.

Willie told his therapist about how he met Jennifer, a professional recruiter for a local banking firm. She was interested in Willie and responded to his interest in her by asking him to dinner. They met at a restaurant. Willie noticed that she looked at every man who came in the door. She kept diverting her eyes in the middle of the conversation and then would look back at Willie. Willie wanted her to maintain the conversation and keep her attention on what they were talking about, and he felt annoyed and upset by her behavior.

Willie could have asked, "What's up? You look like you are looking for someone." But he didn't. Instead he hid his discomfort and felt his skin flush. When Willie talked about the incident, his stutter was slightly more pronounced and the skin around his neck turned bright red. When these observations were pointed out to him, Willie easily recognized his pattern of avoiding conflict, his not telling the truth about his feelings and the meaning of his symptoms. Willie could talk about the problem with insight and clarity when he was not in the situation. But when he directly faced a conflict he forgot what he knew, stuffed his feelings, and faded away. Willie said that when the dinner was over, Jennifer gave him a funny look and said good-bye. Willie returned to his house, didn't sleep well that night, and had trouble getting motivated to go to work the next day.

Willie had communicated his anger to Jennifer, but not in a way that she could understand. She felt him pull away but in a subtle way. When she gave him a puzzled look, it was as if she were asking, "What happened?" Willie's nonresponse gave her nothing to go on. Willie's repressed anger limited his availability to her and hurt the chances of their developing a relationship. In time, Willie began to learn to pay attention to his physical sensations. He learned that when his heart pounded or his skin felt flushed and hot, he was probably avoiding an uncomfortable moment of conflict and limiting his life experiences.

This chapter covered some of the many ways anger avoiders experience symptoms of distress. These symptoms are very important messengers, and are our best friend because they are always present when something is amiss. It is not our feelings that create problems. It is when we have feelings about our feelings that troubles begin. Feelings about feelings can lead to suppressing anger and stop the flow of energy that comes to you and is meant to flow through you. When you stop the flow, symptoms of distress appear.

The next chapter looks at the physical part of anger and other feelings. You might be surprised to find out how much your body is the seat of your feelings and why managing your physical reactions is vitally important to changing your behavior and expressing feelings in healthy ways.

# Changing Your Beliefs and Behaviors

Pull out your journal. What ideas in this chapter were new to you? What old ideas were stimulated by what you've read here? Look at your symptoms. In what ways do you express your distress psychologically, behaviorally, and physically? Can you see what triggers your symptoms? Can you see what you might do differently, so you will experience fewer symptoms and express your anger or react to conflict more directly and honestly?

Write out the three-step exercise based on what you've learned about your symptoms.

1. What did you learn to suppress, and how did you learn to suppress it?

2. What are the symptoms and limitations brought into your life by what you've learned?

3. How are you going to handle difficult feelings and conflicted situations now that you are getting control of your own life?

# 4

# the mind in your body: learning to recognize your own emotions

You feel your feelings in your mind and in your body. It takes both. For instance, you cannot feel angry, tense, and explosive in your mind and be completely relaxed in your body. When you are angry, your physiological responses are agitated and elevated. Likewise, if your body is tight and tense and your fingers are tingling, you are probably not feeling peace and bliss in your mind. In fact, your thoughts would probably be racing and you might be feeling upset, fearful, or angry.

The mind and body are intimately linked. Your body provides a physical location and a physiology that allows your mind to experience a range of feelings with a range of intensity. It is as if there are two minds. The mind in your brain knows, or can figure out, what you are feeling and why you are experiencing that feeling, while the mind in your body works on a different basis and operates to ensure your survival. The mind in your brain seeks to understand the world around us. The mind in your body is interested in whether you are safe and will survive or whether you are unsafe, and your survival is threatened.

This chapter will focus on the mind in your body and how it interacts with the mind in your brain. It will describe what happens in your body when feelings are aroused. This chapter will look at the body from two perspectives: first it will look at what actually happens on a physical basis, and then it will look at how these processes feel to you when they are occurring. One is an objective description of body processes. The other is a subjective experience. For instance, you don't feel an imbalance of the serotonin levels in your brain. That is an objective, physical phenomenon. You feel depressed. That is the subjective experience. This chapter will also look at how you can use your awareness of this mind in your body to help you identify your feelings, both those you are aware of and those you stuff or repress. Even when the mind in the brain fails to register feelings, the mind in the body always registers feelings. It can never fail you. It's designed to sense and react to danger or safety.

When you learn to recognize the signals from the mind in your body, you will be more able to understand your feelings and react in more effective and more organized ways. You can marshal your resources better when you read the signals and integrate what you feel with what you know. Finally, this chapter will describe a specific technique to help you develop the skills to find healthy expression for your feelings. As you will see, there are some basic techniques that can help integrate what you feel with what you know, to respond in an effective manner.

## The Mind in the Body

Your body provides the biochemical and physiological changes that allow you to experience feelings. But the way your body does this can be so powerful that you end up behaving destructively before you can think clearly. When your body is aroused, your thinking can be influenced more by your impulsive reactions than by your conscious intentions. An idea that will help illustrate this comes from Father Martin (1982). Father Martin has helped thousands of people recognize and recover from alcoholism, and is well-known for his lively and captivating talks. In one of his talks he draws an equation on a blackboard and describes how normal, rational functioning can be characterized by the equation I/E.

In this equation "I" stands for our intellectual reasoning and "E" stands for our emotions. Father Martin's model incorporates both our thinking and our feelings. This equation reflects a balanced integration of our thoughts with our feelings, our reasoning and intellect with our emotional arousal. Ideally, healthy human functioning incorporates how we feel with how we choose to behave. We understand what we feel, why we feel that feeling, and how strongly we feel, and then decide how to respond in a way that reflects our personality, our values and ideals, and our beliefs. We have our feelings, but we decide, with our intellects, how to respond to various situations. But we don't always manage problems this well. Sometimes people are impaired by any one of a number of causes.

Father Martin demonstrates this impairment by inverting the equation to E/I. He uses this equation to describe what happens when a person's functioning is influenced by alcohol. He describes how the person's emotions do the thinking and lead the way; the intellect is subject to the person's emotions. Anyone who has experienced difficulties with alcohol will recognize this condition and its unhealthy outcomes. The choices people make and the behaviors they decide to employ are not as rationally driven as before. People can act in impulsive, hurtful, and other unhealthy ways, and then later frequently say, "What was I thinking when I did that?" or "How could I have behaved in that manner?"

## "E" and Anger

Father Martin's model can apply to other situations as well, including anger and rage. Indeed, the equation I/E is a simple way to appreciate how healthy functioning requires an integration of our intellectual and emotional functioning. But when our brains are soaked in "angry neurotransmitters" and our bodies are pumped up with adrenaline for a fight-or-flight response, our functioning can be described not just as E/I, but frequently as E/i.

Here the small case "i" reflects how our behavior can become quite irrational, extreme, and even dangerous when our reasoning or our intellect is impaired or otherwise out of commission. This occurs when we act without thinking, or when we act impulsively, on emotion only, and without reason. Anger avoiders fear they will become anger exploders because they fear their functioning will be reduced to E/i. Anger exploders frequently experience this E/i phenomenon and behave in ways they later regret.

Your body is the primary source of your emotions, as you will soon see. Your brain provides your intellectual reasoning. To balance and integrate your intellect with your emotions, you need to be able to manage and direct your body as well as your mind. When either your intellect or your emotions operate in isolation, or in complete control of the other, your life is impaired. Pure intellectual functioning can solve problems and apply reason, but it can also feel dry, empty, colorless, and boring. Pure emotional functioning can be lively, invigorating, ecstatic, and hilarious, but it can be out of control and without direction or meaning.

This chapter will show you what is happening in your body that can lead you to functioning characterized as E/I, or out-of-control behavior. This behavior is driven by very powerful forces but can be managed by some surprisingly simple techniques. You will learn how to manage the physical power of your feelings and return your functioning and behavior to I/E. This involves a purposeful integration of your feelings with your thoughts and results in your best approach to conflict, anger, or other difficult situations. It takes both your mind and your body to create problematic behavior. And it takes both to produce healthy behavior.

# Mind and Body Connections

Your mind and your body are connected, each influencing the other. This connection leads to specific techniques that can help you manage intense physiological reactions without suppressing the expression of your anger. What is presented here is only meant to be a very simplified and cursory overview of how the mind in the body operates. The point here is to convey a respect for the power and the complexity of our physical responses to feelings. There are three reasons for taking this time to understand how your mind and body are intimately connected.

1. You experience the physical sensations you have in your body when you experience strong feelings and need to respond in a healthy manner.

2. You can find a way to control and direct your responses when you know what your physical responses are and what they mean.

3. Your body provides you with an immediate way to ground and center yourself, and takes you out of the

chaos you feel when your fight-or-flight response is aroused. Your body can be both the beginning of troubled behavior and the beginning of purposeful, directed behavior.

It is no coincidence that you feel physically tense or have other sensations in your body when you feel intense feelings. Your entire body is wired to feel emotions. In fact, 98 percent of emotional receptor cells are in the body, and only 2 percent are in the brain (Polce-Lynch 2002). That is an amazing figure. No wonder we experience butterflies in the stomach, trembling fingers, or other physical reactions when we are angry. We think in our heads, so we tend to assume the seat of our consciousness is in our heads. But we live in our bodies and rely on our bodies for survival. It makes sense that we also "think" with our bodies.

When the mind in your brain thinks, you take in information, make some kind of sense of it, and formulate a reaction to it, spoken or unspoken. The mind in your brain does this primarily in a verbal language. The mind in your body does this same process in a physical language. You take in information and your body develops a sense of safety or danger, pleasure or pain, or comfort or distress. The physical language of the body primarily involves activating a system to alert and protect you or a system to help you relax and calm down. Feelings are directly connected to awareness of safety and awareness of threat. Your body's language is in the form of physical reactions to emotional states that are triggered by events that create threats to your sense of safety.

# Physiology, or What Your Body Is Doing When You Are Angry

This section will be brief and very general in nature. It reviews the physical events your body produces when you experience threats. You don't directly experience these reactions. No one ever says, "I think my amygdala is really acting up today," or "What was that that just passed through my hippocampus?" or "I think my cingulate gyrus is overloaded this morning." You do not experience physiological reactions. You experience the subjective reactions to them. So here's a simplified version of complex physiology.

In Father Martin's terms, the "I" is not just in your brain. It is specifically your *prefrontal cortex*, the part of your brain associated with thinking and reasoning. The "E" is a combination of your *limbic system* and your autonomic nervous system. The limbic system is those parts of the brain associated with emotions and arousal. The *autonomic nervous system* regulates your body's reactions, making you ready to fight or run, or helping you calm down and relax.

But there's more to your physical reaction than simply "I" or "E," or your prefrontal cortex and your limbic and autonomic nervous systems. Your autonomic nervous system regulates many of your reflexive physical reactions. These are the reactions you don't have to think about; they occur automatically. The autonomic nervous system has two components, the sympathetic nervous system and the parasympathetic nervous system. The *sympathetic nervous system* stimulates the fight-or-flight response. The *parasympathetic nervous system* activates the relaxation response. One keys us up; one calms us down. The sympathetic nervous system speeds up your heartbeat, increases blood flow to your muscles, and increases blood pressure and respiration. All of these events function to activate you to take action to protect yourself. The parasympathetic nervous system slows down your heart rate and blood pressure, and helps you breathe slower and deeper. This helps you rest, relax, and recover.

You need both of these systems. If either one dominated your functioning, you would be grossly out of balance. If you only aroused the fight-or-flight response, or the sympathetic nervous system, you would expend all of your energy in intense, exhausting, and ineffective efforts. If you only aroused the relaxation response, or the parasympathetic nervous system, you would get very little accomplished.

So the "E" in Father Martin's equation is connected to a vast array of organ systems and processes in your body. In addition to physical organs, there are different messengers and receptors for those messengers in each organ system. The limbic system is comprised of several structures in the brain: the amygdala, cingulated gyrus, thalamus, hypothalamus, and the interconnections between these structures. These structures are as complex as their names.

The limbic system activates the autonomic nervous system, specifically the sympathetic nervous system for arousal and the parasympathetic nervous system for relaxation. The body uses the *endocrine system,* composed of nine glands—the adrenals, thyroid, parathyroid, pituitary, hypothalamus, pineal, pancreas, testes, and ovaries—to send signals to various muscles and internal organs to fire you up or calm you down. The endocrine system uses hormones and neurotransmitters as messengers to send these signals to your internal organs and muscles. The endocrine system produces the hormones that are carried through the bloodstream or the lymph system to reach the organs in the body that activate the fight-or-flight response or the relaxation response. Internal organs and the autonomic nervous system are full of receptor sites to receive these messengers and respond accordingly. Messenger chemicals, in the bloodstream or in the lymph system, communicate stress, distress, or pleasure to all parts of your body.

Basically, the mind in the body is very active, complex, and interconnected. When you are aware of feeling anger, every cell in your body is affected directly or indirectly. Anger, or any other feeling, is a total mind and body state. You can't feel anger, sadness, fear, joy, or pleasure without a body to feel it in, and a physiology to arouse the body to that feeling state. Feelings are as much a physical state as they are a mental or psychological state.

# The Mind in the Body Is Powerful

You can begin to appreciate how powerful an experience these feeling states can be. There are stories told about mothers who lifted a car off their child when the child was pinned underneath. Perhaps you have personal experiences or have heard stories of incredible feats of strength, speed, or agility when someone was in a dangerous situation. What the human body can do is amazing. Perhaps you can also see how Father Martin's inverted equation, or E/I, can apply to anger and rage as well. The mind in your body can get so agitated, so aroused, and wield such power that you can act in aggressive, dangerous ways, or completely shut down and withdraw, even when these are not logical or healthy responses. Sometimes your body takes over and does your thinking for you. After all, remember, the mind in your body doesn't discriminate between a saber-toothed tiger and an angry spouse. All it knows is that you feel unsafe and need your fight-or-flight response to protect you.

These physical reactions involving the limbic system and the autonomic nervous system occur naturally. They do not require the mind in your brain to start them or tell them when and how to react. The mind in your body reacts naturally and immediately when you experience threats, joy, pleasure, or any other important sensation. This is good to know. Your body is hardwired to act and react to protect you before you realize you need to act or react. In terms of anger management, you need to know how to respond to the signals that you are feeling threatened, so that you can organize your thinking and respond appropriately. Otherwise you can respond in Father Martin's E/I manner, or in the metaphor of the commander and the outpost, like the overexcited messenger sent to solve the problem.

## The Mind in the Body Cannot Mislead You

Your physical system cannot lie to you. Your body will only react when it feels threatened. It will not react when it does not feel threatened, and it will not withhold a reaction when it does feel threatened. Your body always tells the truth. If you can pay attention to and trust your body, you can go a long way toward dealing with your feelings in healthy and effective ways. The next section will name and describe the subjective experiences encountered when you are feeling a feeling. The purpose of this section is to raise your awareness of your own body responses. Again, your body is powerful and truthful. It is powerful enough to give you physical energy to do what you need to do to protect yourself. It is truthful in that your body always reacts to perceptions of threat or experiences of joy. But your body cannot do your thinking for you, and does not discriminate one kind of threat from another. Nor does your body supply you with solutions to problems. It only gives you energy to produce a solution. You must learn to read your body's responses, know what they mean, and find a way to incorporate those responses into an effective problem-solving approach. That takes the cognitive mind, the mind in your brain. Too often we ignore or misinterpret signals from our body and under- or overreact as a result. You can learn to recognize signals from your body that you are reacting to something. In terms of anger management, this also means helping you recognize when you are most likely avoiding anger.

Harris County Public Library
Cy-Fair College Branch
281-290-3210

**Customer ID:** \*\*\*\*\*\*\*\*\*\***9651**

Title: Harness your dark side : mastering j
ID: 34028069357078
**Due: Wednesday, September 11, 2013**

Title: When anger scares you : how to overc
ID: 34028057781008
**Due: Wednesday, September 11, 2013**

Total items: 2
8/28/2013 6:25 PM

Items due by date shown
Please retain this receipt
Renew vis telecirc 713-747-476
or online at www.hcpl.net

rage7, 9 bottom, 10
30, 33, 34 scat, 36 top
44 58, 71 bottom
I/E

## What Do Feelings in Your Body Feel Like?

We generally don't pay attention to the actual physical and physiological responses in our bodies. You don't suddenly become aware that your sympathetic nervous system has become active, or that your amygdala is flooded with activating neurotransmitters or hormones from your endocrine system. What you experience is more immediate and basic than that. You feel physical differences in your body. These differences can feel safe or unsafe, pleasurable or unpleasurable, understood or confusing and disorienting. These physical responses can help you become more focused and pay attention to your immediate situation, or they can be disorienting and distracting. They can help you function better or they can leave you impaired and unable to function at your best.

When you have physical responses to threats and your fight-or-flight response is activated, you feel changes in your body. How and what you feel is completely unique to you. In other words, only you feel what you feel and only you can evaluate how you experience what you feel. But nevertheless there are some commonly shared experiences that come with the physical changes discussed above. Here is a brief list of subjective experiences that can tell you when you are feeling and dealing with emotional experiences, whether you know it or not. These are the subjective experiences that tell you that you are having a strong emotional reaction and that your body may be having a reaction before you know what you are reacting to:

+ flushed skin

+ rapid breathing

+ shaking hands or other muscle tremors

+ sudden dry throat when you are trying to talk

+ stuttering

+ not being able to finish a sentence

+ panic attacks

+ shivering when it's not cold

✦ feeling like your heart is going to burst through your chest

✦ tightness in your neck, chest, or other parts of your body

✦ pain in your stomach, neck, chest, head, forehead, or other parts of your body

✦ sudden or sharp twinges in your neck, back, chest, or arms

✦ butterflies in your stomach

✦ sweating when it's not hot

✦ hot skin

✦ cold skin

✦ skin turning blue

✦ skin turning red

✦ stopping your breathing

✦ irregular breathing

✦ feeling dizzy

✦ feeling faint

✦ blurred vision

✦ feeling like your head is spinning

✦ ringing noise in your ears

Did you notice that all of these signals appear in the body? These are the signs that you are feeling a feeling and your body knows it and is reacting to it. It makes sense that you feel these sensations in your body; after all, 98 percent of the emotional receptor sites are in your body, not in your brain. You don't *think* you have these responses; you actually have them. Paying attention to your body can help you identify feelings. When you are feeling unsafe, threatened, joyful, pleasure, or any other feeling, your body feels it with you, and frequently it feels the feelings before you do.

There are many more subjective reactions than those in the list above. No list could be exhaustive. Which ones listed here do you experience? What do you experience that is not on this list? What can be some of your signals that you are feeling and reacting to important information or threats and need to organize your thinking and reactions so that you don't act impulsively or withdraw out of habit? The more reactions you can identify, the more signals you can use to identify situations where you need to pay attention to what you are reacting to and organize what response you really want to produce.

# Benefits of the Mind-Body Connection

Understanding the mind-body connection can help you identify and control your responses. As you have seen, your body reacts to threats instantly and without error. To demonstrate this, imagine you are sitting in a chair reading this book, and there is a sudden, very loud noise outside the window. Your body will react instantly by jumping and may make your heart pound, rushing blood to your muscles to move you out of harm's way instantly. This happens before your mind can say, "Oh, that was someone slamming their car door." Your body would respond to the experience of a threat (by activating the sympathetic nervous system) before your mind could evaluate whether the threat was real or not, and exactly what the threat was. Similarly, your body can calm down (by activating the parasympathetic nervous system) faster than your mind can calm down. In most situations, your body reacts faster than your mind does.

Our intellect and our emotions influence each other. Our emotional arousal can affect our thinking and reasoning. Our thinking and reasoning can influence our emotional arousal. In the story about Ed and Tony in chapter 2, the way Ed thought about the teasing he received from his family was different from how Tony thought about the teasing he received from his. For Ed, it produced a fun and happy arousal because he liked it when his family got together and told funny stories. Ed's fight-or-flight system did not get aroused. His relaxation response was more active. For Tony, the same teasing aroused a very negative response. He felt threatened by the teasing, and his limbic system responded with negative arousal. He was aroused in a fight-

or-flight manner. He certainly wasn't relaxed. In each case, emotions and intellect exerted an influence on how the event was processed and on how the emotional and intellectual reaction was experienced by each person.

## Body-Mind Technique to Regain I/E Functioning

Since your body cannot lie and reacts faster than your mind can, it makes sense to pay attention to the signals that your body gives you. But then what? Well, you can use the same principle to help you organize and direct your behavior. Since your body responds faster, it can calm you down faster too. So you can use special techniques to calm your body. But calming your body without redirecting your brain only delays the same old pattern. For instance, you may have been told that when you are angry it's better to count to ten before you do or say something. Too often this only delays a destructive or avoidant response. Once you calm your body, you need to give your mind a new task as well. Here is a simple three-step technique that helps.

### Step One: Read Your Body

First, pay attention to the signals. Identify when you are getting worked up. Get to know your body and your constitution and your personality. What are your unique signals? Look over the list of subjective experiences that appeared earlier in the chapter. Think about the last time you felt threatened. What did you experience in your body? Make a list of the physical sensations you felt then.

### Step Two: Calm Your Body

Basically you are activating your parasympathetic nervous system and telling your body that there are no saber-toothed tigers out there and that you are safe from immediate physical attack. You do this by speaking the language of your body and generating relaxation signals. Breathe like you breathe when there are no saber-toothed tigers around: slow and easy. Take several slow deep breaths (they are sometimes called "cleansing breaths"). This tells your body, in its language, that you are safe and the fight-or-flight response is no longer needed. You may want to search your body and find any remaining signals, such as tight muscles in your neck or back, or tenseness in your arms or chest, and loosen up. Flap your arms, wiggle your neck, or swing your arms. Do what it takes to return your body to normal functioning, or to its rest state. This can take ten seconds to a couple of minutes, depending on your skill level and how agitated your body is. The more you practice this, the easier it gets and the faster you will learn to calm and relax your body.

## Step Three: Redirect Your Mind

Redirecting your mind means that you give it a specific set of instructions and a goal. You've told your body there's no saber-toothed tiger out there. You gave your body this message in the language of the body. Now you have to speak to your mind in its language and give it logic, reasoning, goals, and clear directions. This part of the exercise allows you to integrate both your feelings and your thoughts into an effective approach to conflict or other problems. It helps you regain control of your behavior and respond in a way that is neither avoidant nor explosive. You can redirect your mind by speaking the primary language of your mind: words. Words are powerful. When adults use words to redirect or comfort themselves, it is called *self-talk*. Self-talk is using specific phrases or words to help you calm and redirect yourself. It is helpful to have a couple of phrases that you choose or construct beforehand. Memorize or write them down. Then after you have calmed your body, say them to yourself when you are in a conflict. Here are some examples. You could use one or more of these, or use the ideas and develop your own phrases to help you in your unique situation. For instance, you might say:

✦ "I don't have to be afraid; I have something important to say."

✦ "She's angry at me, but she's not going to kill me or end the relationship, and I can calm down and listen to her."

✦ "This is my teenage daughter, not my screaming mother. I can handle her without losing my cool."

✦ "This is important to me, and I can tell him about it in my clear and strong voice."

✦ "I care enough to tell her the truth, even if it's uncomfortable."

✦ "I can get through this moment without running away from it."

✦ "I deserve to be heard as much as she does."

✦ "I don't have to win the argument. I just have to speak my mind clearly."

✦ "My body was racing and I calmed it down. Now I can use my mind to make myself understood."

✦ "This isn't my whole life. It's just one argument with my spouse."

✦ "It doesn't matter if she ends up liking me or not. She's my secretary, not my mother. I can treat her with respect and firmness."

✦ "I can be gentle and strong."

✦ "I can be compassionate and still hold this person accountable for their actions."

✦ "I can be effective and clear without being rude."

✦ "I can speak my mind without losing control."

✦ "I can set limits without being mean or hurtful."

✦ "I can talk with him without screaming or hitting."

✦ "This is important enough to me to take a risk and speak my mind."

✦ "I can feel threatened without acting threateningly."

✦ "She's screaming, but I'm still okay, even if I feel scared or if I think it's all unfair."

✦ "I can be angry and be in control of what I say and do."

✦ "I can say that I'm angry without being a bad person."

✦ "I am uncomfortable with this conflict, but I can work my way though it slowly and clearly."

✦ "I can be polite and still differ with what he is saying."

✦ "I never feel good about myself when I don't speak up for myself."

✦ "I can think of this as a problem to be solved, not a do-or-die situation."

✦ "I can be sensitive to her feelings and still have my own perspective."

✦ "I can handle this conflict. I don't always have to rely on consensus."

The list could go on and on. What are the things to say or remember that would best help you when you are trying to change your behavior and express anger in healthy ways? Are they on this list? What would you add to this list? Can you see how saying these things to yourself after you've calmed your body down could help you redirect yourself and effectively change your approach to uncomfortable situations? Try it and see!

Note: Redirecting your mind is a powerful and effective thing to do, but you can only do it after you've calmed your body. Without relaxing your body, your mind can only continue the fight-or-flight thinking that it produces when your body is fully geared up and not feeling safe. You can redirect yourself in any way that is appropriate for you in that situation, as long as it reflects the values, principles, and decisions that you want to convey.

## Goals of the Mind-Body Approach

This chapter has covered a lot of information. To recap, the mind and the body are intimately linked, especially in the way we process emotional information. Most of our initial responses are in the body, which responds with a fight-or-flight response when we experience something that makes us feel unsafe. The body cannot lie about this; when we feel unsafe, we feel unsafe. It's as simple as that. You've seen that the body contains a vast system of responders, and that we are hardwired for this reaction—it's a part of our survival mechanism. You've seen that your mind can influence your body and that your body can influence your mind. If you can calm your body and initiate a relaxation response, you can change your thinking more effectively.

## Integrating Both Minds

Father Martin's equation shows how important it is to integrate your mind with your emotions in order to have healthy living habits. You have a mind and a body, and both are intimately involved in your emotions and your behavior. Each influences the other. You need to use both your mind and your body when you express anger or any other strong emotion.

If you only used your mind when you expressed anger, it would be a dispassionate and empty experience. If you only used your body, you would constantly react as if you were in life-threatening situations. Neither by itself could capture both the intensity of your feelings and the strength of your convictions. Neither is sufficient, but both are necessary. As you can see from this chapter, integrating your body sensations with your feelings and your thoughts can help you develop skills that will promote healthy conflict, solve problems, and improve and change your behavior in stressful situations. In chapter 7, we will examine healthy expressions of anger and look at specific situations where individuals had to pull together all the ideas presented in this book to handle angry or conflicted situations.

First, chapter 5 examines the question of how anger avoiders learn to avoid. Once you understand the original patterns, avoidant or explosive behavior in adulthood begins to make more sense. And hopefully, once it makes more sense, it is easier to let go of what is no longer useful, and develop new and more effective ways to handle conflict. Chapter 6 takes a close look at two anger avoiders' experiences, to put a human face on the inner struggle that anger avoiders experience on a daily basis.

# Changing Your Beliefs and Behaviors

Okay, before continuing, pull out your journal again. What new ideas did you learn? What old ideas were refreshed? Make a list of the ideas that are important, helpful, or applicable to you.

Now write out your three-step exercise.

1. What in your physical arousal and reactions do you think contributes to your avoidance of anger?

2. How has this limited or affected your life?

3. What will you do now that you are regaining control of your life?

# 5

## origins of anger avoiders

As children we soak up information about our world, its rules, its assumptions, and its expectations. This learning process is both powerfully effective and invisible. How we absorb information from our families of origin is so subtle the process can escape our attention. It's as subtle as breathing. You can think of the learning you received from your family as *psychological air*. You probably don't think about air very often. Yet you are surrounded by it, live within it, and, fortunately, are fully invaded by it. The air you breathe becomes part of who you are, at least on a physical basis. Similarly, the psychological air that surrounded you as a child became part of you.

## Family Rules

Each family has its own psychological air, which translates to psychological rules, or a set of organized beliefs, attitudes, and assumptions about the process of living that helps family members organize and make sense of their experiences. These basic beliefs are as invisible, yet as penetrating, as air. Like physical air, this psychological air is taken in by all members of the family. Without direct awareness, it is absorbed and fully invades each member's psyche. Family members, especially young ones, are shaped by the family air, or the family beliefs, attitudes, and assumptions. In some families the beliefs seem to support a lifestyle based on an inherent sense of safety and well-being, trust, and the healthy connections made between people by open, honest, and respectful expressions of feelings. In these families, people breathe in a psychological air that says that expressing feelings connects people, that people are basically trustworthy, and that exploring the full expression of yourself is exciting and rewarding.

Other families seem to breathe in an awareness that living is dangerous and uncertain, that in order to be safe, people lead disconnected lives, and that feelings only hurt people. It is as if they learn that feelings are unsafe, that expressing feelings disconnects or breaks relationships, that people and relationships are not trustworthy, and that exploring the full expression of yourself only leads to shame and hurt.

Since these beliefs are like air, they are invisible and difficult to name, organize, or confront. These beliefs become an unconscious template upon which people build lives, relationships, and families. In this manner, the basic, subtle beliefs that uniquely define each family tend to be handed down to future generations, in much the same way that DNA is passed down from one generation to the next. But these beliefs are not cast in stone. Everyone is capable of identifying these themes and choosing which ones to keep and which to discard. Some beliefs are obvious; some are more subtle and pervasive. The overall developmental task in adulthood is to separate and individuate. To separate, we identify the rules, attitudes, and assumptions we grew up with and leave behind the ones we do not wish to continue to live with. To individuate, we develop our own rules, assumptions, beliefs, and attitudes, ones that reflect who we have chosen to be and that reflect the core values we choose to live by. Anger avoiders have the same opportunity to separate and individuate as everyone else. The goal of this book is to help you successfully separate and individuate as an adult and develop a healthy lifestyle.

Anger avoiders frequently come from families whose psychological air conveys a message that, as a rule, conflict is to be avoided. These families construct lives and relationships that convey the assumption that expressing conflicted feelings is either shameful to the self or destructive to others. Such families politely avoid any difference of opinion and never utter a harsh or disagreeable word. Expression of anger violates unspoken family rules and the family air. Anger avoiders may also come from families who are either physically violent or psychologically shaming and critical.

# Characteristics of Anger Avoider Families

Anger avoider families represent polar opposites, the two extremes in the expression of anger, yet they share the common belief that anger is hurtful, dangerous, and disrespectful. One type of family acts out this belief in physically violent or other emotionally destructive behaviors. The other type religiously avoids any expression of conflict or manifestation of anger for fear of the destructiveness or shame that could be the only outcome. The following continuum characterizes family comfort with and acceptance of anger. Anger avoiders come from the families at the two extremes of the continuum.

| Overly polite or avoidant families | Families with healthy expressions of conflict | Physically or emotionally explosive families |
|---|---|---|

In real life, this is a continuum, not a set of categories. Any given family may show some characteristics of all three kinds of families but may tend to display more of one pattern than another.

The psychological air in each of these families conveys beliefs, assumptions, and attitudes that pertain to the expression of anger. Although no family has a set of rules written on the walls for all to see, it's possible to deduce some of the unwritten rules. Here are some examples of the unwritten rules in each type of family.

## *Families with Healthy Expressions of Conflict*

✦ Anger isn't scary.

✦ Expression of feelings connects people.

+ Resolving conflicts makes you feel safe.

+ Relationships can contain both safety and conflict.

+ You can love someone and be angry at them for specific reasons.

+ If you care about someone, you name the problem so you can resolve it.

+ The only acceptable and real outcomes are ones that respect each person.

+ People want to stay in relationships and solve problems.

+ People are trustworthy.

+ Feelings are safe and natural and acceptable.

+ Everyone understands and respects others' efforts to explore themselves.

+ Fights and conflicts are normal parts of relationships and living together.

+ Being wrong isn't shameful. It's okay to make a mistake.

+ Anger doesn't make things worse.

+ Everyone basically wants to cooperate and help each other.

## Physically or Emotionally Explosive Families

+ Anger is dangerous and violent.

+ Expression of feelings breaks relationships and is only destructive.

+ Conflicts are resolved by winning or losing.

+ Relationships are either safe or conflicted.

+ Anger cancels out love and ends the good times that went before.

+ In all fights, there is a winner and a loser: one who comes out on top and one who is shamed.

+ People run from conflict.

+ People and emotions are not trustworthy.

+ Angry and conflicted feelings are unnatural.

+ Keep yourself in check and don't break the rules, or you will not be accepted.

+ Fights or conflict mean there's something wrong with the relationship.

+ You are either right and safe, or wrong and shamed.

+ Mistakes are not okay.

+ Anger makes anything worse, or worse yet, anger kills relationships.

+ When there's a conflict, it's all your fault.

## Overly Polite or Avoidant Families

+ Anger is dangerous and shameful.

+ Anger is something to fear.

+ Conflict leads to broken relationships.

+ Expression of feelings shames and disconnects people from each other.

+ Either you love someone or you are angry at them.

+ If you care about someone, you don't bring up troubles.

+ Someone's going to get their feelings hurt in a conflict, and that's bad.

+ People run from troubled relationships.

+ Politeness is trustworthy.

+ The only safe feelings are nice feelings.

+ Keep yourself in check or you will step on someone's toes and hurt them.

+ Conflict and fights mean there's something wrong, and that's bad.

+ Being wrong is shameful.

+ Mistakes are not okay.

+ Anger makes anything worse.

+ If there's trouble or conflict, it's all your fault.

Each of these family models has its own psychological air. Since the beliefs and attitudes expressed in the lists above are unstated, they are expressed in behavioral and attitudinal, not verbal, form.

The three stories below show how people can learn patterns of interaction from their families. The first story describes Ed, who came from an emotionally explosive family. The second one is about Sarah, who came from a physically explosive family. And the third story is about Michelle, whose family was overly polite and avoided anger. Each person learned from his or her family how to behave and what to expect from conflict and expression of feelings. Each person took these patterns into adulthood.

## + Ed's Story

Ed was complex. He could be frighteningly timid, incredibly social, and ingratiating, as well as outrageously explosive and attacking. Yet his dominant inner experience was a chronic and overwhelming fear. He sought psychotherapy to help develop coping skills so he could manage an anxiety he feared would leave him incapacitated. Ed described times when he would cry and shake uncontrollably when pulled over for a routine traffic violation. He feared that any communication from his employer indicated he was being fired, even though he produced more sales than anyone in the region. Ed feared for his life whenever he thought anyone was angry at him.

Yet no one knew this about Ed. He hid his inner fears behind very well-versed social skills. Ed came across as personable and polished, and could make acquaintances and friends feel special and at ease. He always remembered holidays and birthdays with small but thoughtful gifts. He was well liked and seen by others as happy, well adjusted, and pleasantly gregarious. To those around him, it looked like Ed moved through his life with grace and pleasantness, and without an enemy in the world. Even though Ed was never physically violent in his life, and in fact would immediately cower and shiver if ever directly challenged, when Ed blew, he really blew.

Ed's voice and demeanor would change from pleasant to attacking. His face would turn from ingratiating to rageful. He would scream, "Who do you think you are?!" and say to the target of his rage, "I'm going to put you in your place!" Thus, Ed had only two responses to conflict. Most often he would placate, cower, or otherwise retreat. His other response was to explode in a verbal rage.

Ed fit the description of an anger avoider. The psychological air in his family of origin was emotionally explosive. His family was built around psychologically shaming each other.

Ed was frequently beaten up by the school bullies. He quickly learned to hide this from his father, who expressed contempt that Ed didn't just "kick their butts." Ed's father was a prominent businessman who was focused on comparing his success with that of others. He presented himself as a man's man and used material and social status as a way to establish and maintain his dominance. Appearances and acceptance in social circles were very important to Ed's father. He compared Ed to other kids and feared Ed's frailty reflected poorly on him as a man. Ed's father seemed oblivious to the fact that Ed was smaller, weaker, and more insecure than other boys his age. Ed felt ashamed of himself and knew he was a failure in his father's eyes. His father showed contempt for Ed's weakness, and he expressed rage over Ed's fearful behavior. These were his father's main communications to him.

Ed's mother lived in unspoken fear and anger. She deeply resented her husband's hypermasculine attitude and dominance of her. Yet she had no power. She depended on him for all financial and material needs. Over time, Ed's mother found her power. It was in the form of punishing migraines. She would scream, "Look what you've done! Now I have a splitting headache. You're killing me!" and retreat in all her wounded omnipotence to her bedroom. Ed's father was rarely around, and when he was, he didn't pay much attention to her. So Ed's mother exercised her power on Ed and his sister. Any behavior or misbehavior could easily result in what seemed like lethal injuries to his mother. Ed learned to feel very badly about himself. He was told so often, "There's something wrong with you!" that he came to believe it. Both his father's reactions and his mother's message reinforced that belief.

Ed learned a great deal from his family. From his family, he learned the importance of presenting a polished social image. He learned the importance of material success and how to climb the social ladder. But mostly Ed learned shame, a violent and invading shame that overwhelmed him and drove him inside himself. Even though he was a success by any measure, inwardly Ed knew he was weak, a failure, and an impostor. What he showed others was a polite image, but Ed's inner world was much less polished. When he was angry, Ed immediately became fearful. It was as if anger didn't exist for him; only fear existed. Yet when he did feel anger, it was expressed as his parents' rage at him had been expressed: powerful, haughty, shaming, hurtful, and echoing the messages thrust upon him: "What's the matter with you! Look what you've done to me!" Ed avoided all anger when he felt unsafe, and exploded in shaming rages when he felt safe. When he felt unsafe, Ed behaved as most anger avoiders do; he feared any expression of anger. But when he felt safe and was not inhibited or under immediate threat, he behaved with the only other pattern he knew: Ed exploded. Ed was either totally vulnerable or totally invincible. His style of expressing anger mirrored this.

## ✦ Sarah's Story

Sarah was the violent partner, not her husband, Doug. Doug's family abandoned him to foster care. After four or five new homes, he learned to be quiet and not react to trouble. Sarah was another story. She was physically violent with Doug and had two voices, normal and screaming. Like many couples, they had troubles early in their relationship. Doug hid from it. Sometimes he'd go to the shed and busy himself with some project. Sometimes he just didn't come home. Sarah's temper was the same, regardless of the trigger. If Doug overspent the budget, left late for work, didn't do his share of the chores, or left a mess in the bathroom, Sarah went ballistic. It was as if she had no in-between response.

Anger avoiders and anger exploders reflect basically the same approach to anger. Sarah rejected an anger avoider approach because she thought of herself as tough.

So she behaved with the only alternative known to her. She was an anger exploder.

Sarah and Doug sought counseling to avert a separation. The counselor asked Sarah where she learned to respond in this manner. She hadn't thought of it as a learned pattern. In fact, she secretly felt badly about herself for acting this way but never said so. After a while, Sarah came out with stories of a violent and alcoholic home, always in chaos and always out of control. There was no moderation in any aspect of Sarah's family. Drinking, punishment, and yelling all were taken to extremes. Once a teacher thought Sarah threw chewing gum at another student. It was actually the girl behind Sarah. But Sarah's parents were called when Sarah protested the teacher's accusations. Sarah said she could still see her father's raging face, hear the derogatory names he called her, and feel the physical punishment he doled out. Sarah didn't soften as she told the story. She remained as angry at the incident as if it had just happened. She didn't cry or feel sad about how she had been treated. She had only one response—intense anger—the same anger Doug experienced in the house.

A lot of pain, tears, and terror lay behind Sarah's anger, but she kept this well hidden from others and herself. Sarah would need to learn about having other feelings. She had never been able to feel afraid or sad in her family. She had to defend herself instead. It was as if blind rage were the only emotion anyone in her family felt or experienced. As an adult, Sarah did the same.

### ✦ Michelle's Story

Michelle was bright, competent, deliberate, and soft-spoken. She talked in a slow, thoughtful manner and seemed never to lose control. She was very successful. After a few years of running her own business, she had several employees. Michelle dressed in a stylish yet businesslike manner. At first appearance she seemed a competent, confident woman. Why was she seeing a therapist? Ironically, Michelle was asking for help solving a problem she knew how to solve.

Michelle's husband floundered in his blue-collar job as much as she succeeded in her white-collar career. This meant little to Michelle. She had been married for a long time and had no desire to divorce. She understood that her husband felt threatened and feared she would leave him for someone better. Michelle knew he felt uncertain about himself and his career and that he feared he was inadequate for her. Michelle didn't flaunt or flout her success. Rather she was quiet and matter-of-fact about it. Michelle sounded like an understanding, nonthreatening spouse—polite, thoughtful, and easy to get along with.

What was the problem? Michelle said that her husband was controlling and occasionally threatened her. He had tried to limit her contact with church and community groups where she liked to volunteer. He limited their travel and timed her shopping trips. If she was gone longer than expected, he'd go out looking for her or call the store to see if she was still there. He hated it when she visited friends, so Michelle usually relented and stayed home. Michelle said he got angry easily and would yell and scream at her to control her activities and contact with other people. When he drank, he would physically grab her to prevent her from going anywhere.

When her therapist asked Michelle how she felt when her husband acted in these ways, she responded, "I think he's insecure and afraid of losing me." Michelle showed a generous understanding of her husband's fears and the human motivation behind his inhuman behaviors. She knew he loved her dearly and that he was not trying to hurt her, but rather was trying to protect himself. When the topic was probed further, Michelle added, "I think this is the kind of stuff that goes on in lots of marriages, especially when the men don't have anyone to talk to and are afraid their wives have lots of people to talk to."

Michelle was calm, thoughtful, and compassionate as she spoke of this. Then, she added, almost as an afterthought, "Just like my mother." This was the first hint of what her husband's behavior meant to Michelle. When asked to elaborate, Michelle said, "My mother lived with my father's drinking and yelling. She was a college graduate and wanted her own career but got pregnant right away and became a housewife instead." Michelle described how her mother assumed it was a woman's place in life to put up with and take care of her husband. In spite of her mother's sobriety and intelligence, she never confronted her father or exercised her personal power to tell him to stop his destructive behavior.

Somehow Michelle felt she would betray her mother, and violate an unspoken standard about being a good wife if she stood up to her husband and took control of her own life. The real problem wasn't her husband's behavior, in spite of how awful his behavior was to her. The problem she was asking for help with was within herself. She needed to come to terms with what anger and confrontation meant to her. From her mother, Michelle had learned that wives don't get angry or confront. But this rule didn't work in Michelle's life anymore.

Michelle described a close relationship with her mother and said that she had learned a great deal from her. Michelle could vividly remember the graceful ways her mother handled problems. Her mother never lost her temper and always seemed to rise above the problems. Michelle loved her mother and felt profoundly safe in her presence. When her father drank or yelled, Michelle's mother would tell Michelle about the hard days her father experienced, the personal and business setbacks he faced, and the trouble he felt. Michelle had begun to see and understand her father the same way her mother did, in a very kind, understanding, and humanistic manner. What was missing was corrective action. Michelle's mother constantly adapted to his behavior, but never said, "Stop!" or "You can't talk to me like that, even if you did have a bad day!" Like her mother, Michelle was very loyal to relationships and had a keen understanding of her husband. Like her mother, Michelle had left herself out of the picture and adapted to the situation instead of confronting her husband.

# Family Legacies

There are clear but subtle and unstated attitudes, beliefs, and assumptions in each family described in the stories above. These attitudes, beliefs, and assumptions form patterns of interaction. In such patterns as these, anger avoiders learn how to behave and what to expect from others. Anger avoiders learn important and powerful messages from their families of origin about relationships and expression of feelings in general, and specifically about anger. These patterns are passed down from one generation to the next.

But it is the task of each generation to separate and individuate from the previous generation. Each generation must carry on healthy family traditions and rituals, and develop new and healthy ones to replace unhealthy patterns. You can separate from family patterns of avoiding, exploding, or shaming as a way of dealing with conflict. You can individuate and develop new and healthy patterns of handling anger and conflict. These healthy patterns can be passed on from generation to generation as well.

In the next chapter, you will see how all the information presented so far feels from a subjective or personal perspective. The voice presented will be the subjective voice, the personal thoughts, feelings, struggles, and doubts experienced by two anger avoiders.

# Changing Your Beliefs and Behaviors

Pull out your journal again. What new ideas did you encounter? How would you describe the psychological air in your family? What were the attitudes, beliefs, and assumptions conveyed to you when you were young? Was your family physically explosive, psychologically violent, or avoidant and polite? Did these vignettes remind you of any aspects of your family's functioning?

Use your three-step writing exercise now to help you pull together what you learned in your family's psychological air.

1. What attitudes, beliefs, and assumptions did you learn?

2. How have these attitudes, beliefs, and assumptions limited your life and relationships so far?

3. What will you do differently now that you are getting control of your life?

# 6

# a week in the life of
# two anger avoiders

Anger avoiders' lives are made up of the same small stuff that everyone experiences, but their inner lives are colored by their constant avoidance of conflict and the resulting emotional costs. The two diaries in this chapter reveal anger avoidance from the inside, how it feels to be an anger avoider. One is a man's personal diary, the other a woman's. In each, you can hear the inner struggle, the self-talk, and the discomfort that accompanies a week's experience of avoiding anger.

Both people, Jim and Jessica, were in therapy for depression and dissatisfaction with personal and career issues. They were asked to write their thoughts, feelings, and reactions on a daily basis. They were told, "Write as if there were a microphone in your head that could capture the thoughts and feelings that would go unnoticed or would be quickly repressed." For the sake of brevity, entries over the first few weeks of therapy have been collapsed into one week, highlighting events that capture the personal struggles of anger avoiders.

## ✦ Jim's Story

Jim is a forty-three-year-old man, married, with
two children and a career as a computer database
administrator. He initially sought therapy because
he feared he was losing motivation and was neglecting
important tasks at work and at home. Jim described
his health, marriage, and career as solid, and he was
perplexed by his mood. He wondered why he felt
depressed if he had nothing to be depressed about.
Here is Jim's typical week, echoing the themes presented
in the first five chapters.

## ✦ Monday, 8 A.M.

*Monday mornings are rough. I dread them. The kids are still
sleepy from the weekend's play and sleepovers. Maggie is just
hitting puberty. She needs her sleep. Mondays are roughest for
her. Bobby, four years younger, gets cranky but doesn't have the
raw anger and temperament that are Maggie's morning
signatures. This morning she was grumpy when she awoke and
quickly went downhill from there. My "Good morning, Sweetie"
was greeted with, "It's 6:45. I told you to get me up by 6:40!"
and a dark-faced stomp to the bathroom. I know this mood
changes in the next hour or so. By the time she heads off to
school, she is her usual happy self, always leaving with an "I
love you" before she closes the front door. But not now.*

*I struggle with my mood and reactions. Part of me wants
to yell back, "You brat! How dare you talk to me like that!"
I feel so insulted by her lack of gratitude. "Get your own
breakfast, fix your own lunch!" I could bellow, but I withhold
and am uncomfortable. I'm sure there's a way to respond
without inflaming her mood or shaming her into tears. Maggie's
mother can do it. She expresses her anger at Maggie's behavior,
sets the limit, and somehow invites Maggie into the next
moment with her. Not me! My heart is pounding; my muscles
are ready to pounce. I know my temperament would take over.
It's easy to remember the counselor's words, "You can't parent,
which is an endless string of opportunities to teach, when your
body is geared to fight and your mind is revisiting every injustice
you've endured in the last decade. You have to calm your body,
then your mind, and then open your mouth and say something*

*with parental clarity." Boy, that sounds great! But there's Maggie, grumpy and abrasive as only a preteen at 6:40 in the morning can be. Here's me, hurt, angry, and walking away with feelings I'll carry for hours.*

*Maggie and her mother are closer than Maggie and I. They fight better, laugh better, and play better. It seems to me that they know each other better than Maggie and I do. It is evident in the way they are comfortable with each other, even when they are fighting. When I walk away from conflict with Maggie, I wonder if I walk away from a better relationship too.*

*My real fear is that I'll scream before I can think. I fear my own anger will explode all over Maggie. She'll cry and tell me how mean I am. And in my head, I will say to myself, "She's right, you're no better than, and no different from, your father. Where's all that 'I'm not going to treat my kids like that' now?" My thoughts and reactions feel disorganized. I hated it when my father yelled. His anger was so big, and I was so little. I swore I'd never be angry at my kids. Yet here I am, holding back my screams at Maggie.*

*I'll bet my friends' kids don't treat them like this. I'll bet Richard's kids don't even think to say this stuff to him. And if they do, I'll bet Richard handles it right away, without a moment's hesitation, and sets the right limit. What would he think of me if he knew I felt so unsure of myself and didn't handle my daughter any better than this? What would my coworkers think of me if they knew? I don't feel so professional anymore.*

Jim's first response to anger is a predictable fear of exploding. He avoids conflict even when he has a clear right to be angered. Jim becomes physiologically aroused and can't think straight. He fears his pounding heart will lead to destructive behavior, so he withholds and avoids. Later, in a calm body and free from adrenaline, Jim can think clearly and knows what he was supposed to say. Thinking about a correct response actually makes Jim feel worse because he now feels more inept.

Jim knows that his daughter will be grumpy, yet he fears *his* response to *her*. Jim wants to be able to tell Maggie, "I know you feel bad in the morning, but that doesn't mean you can behave badly," just as his wife does, but he fears he'll explode instead. He feels a rush of pumping adrenaline. With his heart pounding, he is unable to use parenting skills that are available to him under less-stressed conditions. He comes from a family of anger exploders. While Jim is committed to not repeating his father's patterns, he lacks healthy alternatives. Jim is limited to "avoid" or "explode" as options.

Jim evaluates himself by comparing himself to his wife and to other men, real or imagined. Men often compare themselves to other men. When anger avoiders do this, it actually increases their fear. Men fear being inadequate in the eyes of other men. While comparing himself to his friend Richard, Jim feels even more inept and incompetent. Jim actually did not yell at his daughter. She went to school in her usual good mood, but Jim felt weak, inept, and incompetent. Jim expresses his anger only at himself.

## ✦ *Tuesday, 9 P.M.*

*It's funny how I can be so good at work, look fine to my coworkers, and feel so uncertain and shaky, all at the same time. I had one of my best days and one of my worst ones today. I finished the data analysis project by devising a new way to collapse and store the data. Even I was impressed with how I accomplished it.*

*Then, at lunchtime, I went to pick up the dry cleaning. There were two people in front of me. The person in front was talking to the cashier about her car trouble. They went on and on. They seemed oblivious to me and the other customer. I wanted to say, "Hey! I don't have all day!" I made shuffling motions and exhaled hard to try to get the cashier's attention. But these two started talking about the work week in Detroit and how cars made during vacation season were always trouble. I was hoping the person in front of me would say something to them. But she just turned and left me in the line. I waited for what must have been twenty minutes. Finally they stopped talking. I thought they were through, and I started to move toward the counter. But then it turned out that the cashier hadn't yet retrieved the customer's clothes and had to go to the back of the store to find the woman's lost skirt.*

*I was so mad! I wanted to yell, or at least say something like, "Don't you care about anything except cars?" I was angry and I felt like being mean. My stomach was in a knot, and I was late for work. But when they finished, I went up to the counter and said, "Hi, I'm here to pick these things up," and handed her the slip for the clothes. I don't want to know what my blood pressure was. When I left the dry cleaner's, the only thing I did was slam the door to my own car.*

*When I returned to work I was still furious! My secretary asked me what was wrong. I said, "Oh, nothing," and went back to my terminal. My stomach was growling now because I hadn't eaten. I wished I had said something at the dry cleaner's. Now I was angry with myself! Why didn't I calmly and firmly tell the cashier that I was on my lunch break and needed to hurry? The words seemed so simple now. Why couldn't I have thought of them when I was in line, fuming. Why couldn't I just take care of the situation with the clarity that came to me later? This made me feel worse. For the rest of the afternoon I was in a funk—angry with myself as well as at the cashier. But I was mostly angry with myself because I had failed to step up to the plate and assert myself.*

Jim had a right to be angry about the events at the dry cleaner's, but all of Jim's internal dialogue was loud and out of control. His body was explosive too. Jim associated anger with the explosive urges he felt, so he spent his energy containing himself instead of solving the problem. Fear of anger froze him in place. He couldn't move toward solving the problem. Jim failed to control his physiological responses. So he succumbed to the survival mentality that fear brings, instead of the problem-solving energy that healthy anger can bring. As he became more upset, he was less able to identify and solve his problem.

## ✦ Wednesday, 9 P.M.

*The boss took me into her office this morning. I wondered what could be wrong. She said I have good ideas and solve problems well, but said I "lead from the rear." She said she wanted me to work on my leadership skills and wanted to talk about a promotion to project manager. I would be in charge of six of my coworkers. She wants me to increase productivity and provide direct supervision to people having trouble with their work. I was flustered and started stammering. My face felt flushed, but she didn't seem to notice. She looked right at me and wanted a response. I told her I'd think about it and quickly left her office. The thought of holding people accountable for their performance rattles me. I can't organize my thinking clearly, but I know I feel unsettled by the idea. She wanted a response by next Friday. I'm not sure what to do.*

Jim faces a challenge common to many anger avoiders. He avoids conflict and confrontation, fearing he will hurt others or not be able to organize his resources to master the situation. Yet he is competent and capable. His natural abilities make him a candidate for advancement to a management position, but his fear keeps him from developing his full potential.

### ✦ *Thursday,* 10 A.M.

*Stacy, my wife, says I am too focused on myself, and I don't think about her and the kids the way I should. It came up this morning when I was talking to her about an addition to the den so I can have a place to develop a consulting business and eventually work for myself. Stacy says what she's thinking and doesn't pull any punches. She made it clear that this isn't the time for me to go off on a new venture. She couldn't see how I could bring it up now. She pointed out that both kids need braces, the car has nearly 200,000 miles on it, and we haven't put anything away for retirement. Then she called me selfish!*

*I know about the car and the braces. The problem isn't my being selfish. We just don't make enough money, and never will unless we change something about our income. I know enough about the computer business to know my own worth on the open market. It's the only way to solve the money problems. But when Stacy started in on me, I got tongue-tied. I heard what she was saying, but I couldn't tell her my thoughts. Something happened. I was speechless and listened to her describe me from her point of view. I couldn't find my own words. I knew what I wanted to say before we got started. But I lost my way once the argument began. It sounded so great when it was in my head: I'd gradually develop more independent consulting contracts, wean myself from the salaried job, and be home more with the kids. We'd have more income and could plan ahead and pay for what we needed. I felt good, like I was doing my job as the main breadwinner.*

*As usual, Stacy made her point and moved on. But I still felt stung, by both her words and my inability to respond to her. I always leave unfinished and don't move on to what comes next. This discomfort stays with me. Later, when the kids were asleep and Stacy wanted to spend time together, I didn't feel as open, close, and trusting as I wanted to be. I know I'm not finished with the conflict and am not ready to*

*be close. She is finished with it and is ready. I end up feeling
more uncomfortable with myself than with her.*

*I realize I was angry, and that was what made me lose
my voice. I didn't like what Stacy was saying. But I lost my
voice when I was angry and didn't know what to say. It's
almost like I was afraid of my own anger, if that's even
possible?! My counterattacks of her "narrow thinking" would
have made things worse. I wish I had a better alternative.*

Again, Jim has difficulty managing his physical reactions.
He gets agitated and ends up frozen. He loses his voice, can't get
his thoughts out clearly, and ends up speechless. These are more
like the symptoms of fear, as described in chapter 3, than anger.
He couldn't think clearly and avoided exploding with counterattacks. Once again, Jim felt frustrated by his own inability to
express anger in a healthy manner.

## ✦ *Saturday, 10 A.M.*

*My friend Richard and I run together once or twice a week. He
always asks, "How are you doing?" Most often, in typical guy
talk, I lie, say "fine," and ask how he is doing. I don't talk
about the week's troubles. Not because of anything dark and
horrible. It's more because I do not know what another man
would think of my struggles and failures. Does he get his point
across with his wife with fairness, clarity, and ease? Does he
handle conflict with aggressiveness, or at least assertiveness?
What would he think if he saw me walk away from Maggie's
morning behavior without a corrective response? What would he
do if it were he in line, late for lunch? Would it be easier for
him to handle his anger in the moment than it is for me?*

*My pattern is so predictable . . . I feel angry, but I don't
act on my anger. I fear I'll hurt someone. So, I retreat,
sometimes under fire, usually without a fight. Later I feel like
I have something to hide. I feel a shame within me. It's not
clear at first. Only when I think about it does it become clear.
I don't stand up. I don't act like a man. I feel different,
somehow less than Richard and other men. I know I'm not
really less than other men. But the feeling haunts me. It colors
my mood and detracts from my accomplishments and joys.
I back away from anger and never feel good when I do.*

*But I don't say this to Richard on our run together, even
though I know I can trust him with these troubles. Instead,*

*I say, "Fine, how are you doing?" I am not as comfortable with Richard as I know I could be. The events of the week affect our relationship too.*

*My days have good times too. This anger issue is not the only thing in my life. But it's there, waiting for me, around the next bend. I am uncomfortable when I am angry. I don't hurt anyone but myself with it, and that hurts!*

Again, men compare themselves to other men. It can be argued that traditional masculinity is maintained in the gaze of other men. Each man worries about whether other men see him as "man enough." Jim compares himself to his best friend, another man, and fears he will not measure up to masculine standards. As you will see in chapter 9, Jim's difficulties are similar to those of other men. Like a well-kept secret, men don't share their experiences. Instead, they compare themselves against "manly" standards and hide their shortcomings.

Jim fears being an anger exploder, so he withholds himself from conflict. He knows this limits his relationships. But he lacks a way to comfortably and effectively express anger. He fears being seen as a failure in his own eyes and in the eyes of other men. Jim's physical experience of anger is intense and disorganizing. Jim needs to understand and manage his physical as well as his emotional reactions. Jim wants to be a good father and husband. Jim does not want to behave like his father, so he keeps his anger inside. When he does this, though, he feels badly about himself. So Jim struggles with low self-esteem. He names himself inept, afraid, and a failure. Then he finds ways to live up to these names.

## ✦ Jessica's Story

Jessica is a thirty-eight-year-old woman, also married, with no children, and employed in human resources for a small company. Jessica sought therapy when her primary care physician suggested some of her constant physical symptoms could be stress related. Jessica had chronic headaches and borderline hypertension. She had trouble sleeping three or four nights per week and had gained twelve pounds in the previous six months. Jessica was somewhat surprised to end up in a therapist's office. After all, she had a good childhood, was never abused, and felt close to her parents, brother, and two sisters.

## ✦ Monday, 5 P.M.

*I can't believe the difference a day makes. Yesterday I was with old friends, relaxed and easy. My friends and I have been together since college. Once a month we go on our Sunday brunch and a shopping tour. It's an easygoing group. No one brings baggage when we're together. It's more like playtime.*

*But work is different. Today I'm facing a roaring lion and my neck is so tense it hurts. My boss has a sharp temper. When he doesn't like something, he pounces on it. I think his motto is "shoot first and ask questions later." This morning he misread my monthly report and went ballistic. He bellowed like an old battle-ax. I felt scared. I was shaking inside and close to tears. My reaction to his anger is always the same. I become frightened and overcompensate to placate him. Later, I am fuming and can't believe he talked to me that way. I wish I could remember I am angry when I'm angry, not hours later, when the whole mess has been worked out. Oh well, maybe it's better this way. No telling what I'd say if I really felt my anger!*

*By the time I stopped shaking, it was midafternoon and he had taken the report to the management team. What gets me even madder is the thirty-six hours that I put into that report and the credit he takes for presenting it. I should have taken the director's position when it was offered to me, but I was too chicken! I couldn't see myself being the warhorse he is. I don't want to write performance evaluations, delegate hard work, and supervise my coworkers.*

*When I get home, I am alone for about an hour before Randy arrives. Even though I spend the entire hour fuming at myself, I don't tell Randy about it. I know exactly what he would tell me about standing up for myself. The truth is, I don't think I'd know what to say to my boss. I can't anger him. He's my boss. It would only be counterproductive. It's best to leave things as they are.*

Like Jim, Jessica is first frozen by the physiology of fear, then later, after the immediate intensity passes, she becomes angry. Jessica feels worse about herself for not handling the incident the way she wished she could. She was inept under fire and masterful only later, when she was alone. Jessica's discomfort with anger may be complicated by her desire to maintain connective relationships. She tries to placate her boss, a relationship maneuver, and fears a director's position because she cannot see how to be authoritative without being adversarial.

### ✦ *Tuesday, 8* A.M.

*I love my husband. He's such a great guy, everything I could ever hope for. We've barely even had a fight! So I feel guilty when I get angry with him. He left the milk and ice cream on the counter all night. It was a mess in the morning. He had to leave early, so he left it for me to clean up. I was confused by my feelings. I was angry and resented that he made the mess and I had to clean it up. Then I felt guilty for being angry, which seems so complicated. But somehow I felt like I was being disloyal to Randy if I was angry with him. "Confused" doesn't begin to describe how I feel. I love him, but I am angry with him. Then I feel like I am a bad person for being angry with him.*

*I wanted to make it all okay, so I cleaned up the mess and tried to act like I wasn't bothered by it. I think he knew something was wrong when I only gave him a glancing kiss this evening when I got home. I still feel badly for being angry, but I don't want to mention it because it seems petty.*

The only purpose of anger is to mobilize people to solve problems. Jessica has normal problems in a normal relationship. Randy's behavior was not purposely intended to create discomfort and conflict for Jessica. But it did. Saying "Randy, I love you, but I'm angry when you make a mess and then leave it for me to clean up. This really bothers me and gets in the way of my being close and intimate with you. Please clean it up!" would address and solve the problem without damaging either of them. Yet Jessica associates anger with destructiveness and assumes a negative outcome will result with expressions of anger. Thinking that she's protecting the relationship, she stuffed her anger. Later her anger remained because the problem remained. Neither went away.

### ✦ *Wednesday 10:30* P.M.

*I never thought today would happen. It all sneaked up on me before I knew it. I didn't sleep well last night. Randy and the ice cream must have still been on my mind. I woke up tired and crabby. It didn't help that Randy left a mess again. I got to work just in time. Before I could even get settled in my office, three people came in with problems and complaints. One coworker had fought with her boyfriend and wanted to tell me about it. I didn't feel like dealing with her tears right then. Next, my supervisor wanted my performance objectives before lunch. Then came the office supply coordinator wanting my list. He's so pushy and demanding. I couldn't take anymore. I blew up at him! Told him to get out of my office and take his stupid supply list with him. His jaw dropped and practically bounced on the floor. He looked more than shocked and started to fire some words back at me. But he saw the look on my face and just turned and left the room. I couldn't believe what had come out of my mouth! I felt so bad. No telling what he thought of me.*

*I don't know why that happened. It isn't like me. I wondered if everyone heard it and what they think of me now.*

Jessica avoided and avoided and then exploded. Anger avoiders' fear of exploding keeps them stuck in avoidance behaviors. Jessica is not aware of her anger. In spite of this, anger influences many of Jessica's reactions. Her fear of destructive exploding becomes a self-fulfilling prophecy when she is overloaded with demands and does not have healthy anger expression skills. Exploding is the only thing left to do. Then Jessica feels bad about herself, fears she hurt someone else, and worries that other people will see her as she sees herself, a bad person.

# ✦ *Thursday,* 9 P.M.

*Not much happened today. I had a splitting headache when I came home and had to take an aspirin and a two-hour nap. The day started out with a surprise. The proposal I turned in yesterday was back on my desk with pages and pages of revisions. I know I had done it correctly, but I had to work on it for hours to fit in the project manager's changes. I don't think it will be accepted by the review board because of these changes. But I didn't say anything. I didn't want to anger the project manager. I had to leave out some of my best ideas. Come to think of it, I completed two proposals this week. In the end, it amounted to nothing. Other than that and my headache, it was a good day.*

Jessica began therapy because of a suggestion that her chronic physical complaints were stress related. Jessica's description of the day is brief and cursory, but her stress appears to be complex. Jessica put her own good ideas aside to comply with the project manager's directives, in spite of her considerable invest-ment of time and effort. She seeks consensus over conflict and cooperation over confrontation when she doesn't stand up for her ideas. She avoids angering another person at her own expense. And because Jessica is not aware of the issues or costs, she devel-ops physical symptoms instead.

## ✦ *Friday, 8 P.M.*

*My mother called today. She was complaining about Dad. I've heard one complain about the other for years. Why they don't just talk with each other, I'll never know. I know they love each other. But each will call my brother or me and sing a litany of familiar complaints. I almost blurted out, "Why don't you talk to Dad instead of me?" but I was afraid I'd hurt her feelings. She talked for an hour. This came after a long week. I really wanted to spend the time with Randy. But, by the time I got off the phone, I was too tired and just went to bed.*

Jessica's last entry is revealing. Whereas Jim came from a family of anger exploders, Jessica's family members are avoiders. It is as if anger and conflict are not polite, and expressions of anger are not acceptable. These family norms are quiet and perva-sive. Jessica abided by the norms. She did not confront her mother and stayed on the phone for an hour, when she wanted to spend the time with Randy. Jessica has difficulties establishing boundaries with her mother, Randy, and her employers. She is known as a loyal, kind, thoughtful, and competent person, but Jessica's unexpressed anger leaks out in her physical ailments.

Avoiding anger has become an ingrained lifestyle for Jessica. She grew up with anger avoiders. Without ever acting in destruc-tive ways, she learned to fear and avoid anger. She works hard, sometimes driven by her fear of other people's anger. Like Jim, her career and relationships are affected by the way she stuffs or ignores her anger. Her psychological pain can occasionally become physical as she lacks other outlets and does not attend to her emotional pain.

In Jim's and Jessica's personal diaries you can hear their pain and discomfort. Both are anger avoiders. Jim is more aware of the effects of avoiding anger than Jessica is. Nevertheless, both expe-rience limitations in their careers and personal relationships. Both suffer in self-esteem and self-confidence. They hold themselves back and live less-productive, less-fulfilling lives than they could have. Jim and Jessica fear anger and avoid "being bad." They are compliant and deferential when they could take more decisive action. Each needs to understand and learn how to express anger in healthy and productive ways. When they do, they will be as compassionate, hardworking, and caring as they are now. They will also feel better about themselves and the actions they take.

# 7

# what healthy anger expressers know: putting it all together

Up to now, this book has focused on the differences between anger and rage. In this chapter you will look at the beliefs, attitudes, and behaviors of healthy anger expressers. These are people who feel comfortable with conflict and expressing anger. They feel safe clearing the air and bringing up what bothers them. They can be blunt at times, but they do not convey disrespect or rudeness. Their friends know where they stand and trust them to be honest and straightforward. That isn't to say that life is easy for them or that they are never uncomfortable with conflict. But they understand that conflict and anger themselves are a necessary and productive part of life, and have to be dealt with just like everything else. Healthy anger expressers face problems and experience failure, doubts, and hesitations just like everyone else does. But they know that the expression of anger does not alienate them from others and does not indicate that they are mean-spirited. If you look at how people express anger in healthy ways, perhaps you can become more familiar and comfortable with healthy anger expression yourself.

# Characteristics of Healthy Anger Expressers

Healthy anger expressers understand or, because of their early learning, take for granted a lot of the concepts and models presented here. Healthy anger expressers breathe a psychological air that conveys many beliefs and attitudes that enable them to feel free and comfortable with conflict. Because they have been expressing anger as a normal part of life for a long time, they have a range of skills and experiences that help them find ways of managing conflict and handling difficult situations without losing their bearings. Healthy anger expressers live in their body and understand the physical signals that tell them they are reacting to something. They do not feel afraid of their feelings, but rather they accept what they feel for what it is. Healthy anger expressers utilize many of the concepts and skills talked about in previous chapters. Let's review some of what has been covered.

## Psychological Air

Healthy anger expressers breathe a different psychological air from anger avoiders. In their families, you will find a comfort and trust with expressing anger and a faith in conflict resolution. In families of healthy anger expressers, you might also find the following attitudes, beliefs, and assumptions embedded in the family rules:

+ Healthy expression of feelings connects people and makes relationships stronger.

+ Relationships can contain both safety and conflict.

+ You can love someone and be angry with them for specific reasons.

+ If you care about someone, you name the problem so it can be solved.

+ The only acceptable and real outcomes are ones that respect each person.

+ People want to stay in relationships and solve problems.

+ People are basically trustworthy.

+ Feelings are safe and natural and acceptable.

✦ Exploring the full expression of self is good.

✦ Fights and conflicts are normal parts of relationships and living together.

✦ Being wrong isn't shameful. It's okay to make a mistake.

✦ Anger doesn't make things worse.

✦ Everyone basically wants to cooperate and help each other.

These are some of the invisible family rules that influence the psychological air that each family lives in and passes on from generation to generation. Individuals in families learn these rules at some level of consciousness and develop individualized attitudes, beliefs, and assumptions about anger and conflict. These rules are equally invisible but nevertheless exert a powerful influence on how each person functions and expresses or withholds expression of self, feelings, and conflict. In other words, healthy anger expressers possess a set of beliefs that enable them to move into conflict instead of away from it.

## Beliefs, Attitudes, and Assumptions

It may be helpful to review some of the beliefs, attitudes, and assumptions that make healthy anger expressers able to manage conflict better. Some attitudes are stated in terms of what anger is not. Some are stated in terms of what anger is.

Here are some statements about anger that healthy anger expressers learn and practice in their daily lives:

✦ Anger is not violent or destructive.

✦ Anger is not harmful.

✦ Anger is not shameful.

✦ Anger does not break or hurt relationships.

✦ Anger doesn't hurt people's feelings.

✦ Anger does not mean you are a bad or unfriendly person.

✦ Anger is not a loss of control.

✦ Anger is not aggressive.

✦ Anger doesn't mean people won't like you.

✦ Anger does not mean you are behaving badly.

✦ Anger is not something to fear.

✦ Anger does not mean yelling or screaming.

✦ Anger does not imply alienation, rejection, or humiliation.

How many of these statements do you believe? How many statements do you believe more now than when you started this book? Has doing some of the exercises in this book changed your attitudes about anger?

## Putting It Positively

Many of the same ideas can be better stated in the positive than in the negative. It's important to state what you've learned to do, in addition to what you've learned not to do. You can't go on with your life simply not believing certain ideas or not behaving in certain ways. You need a way to believe or behave. As you read the following statements, can you see how your beliefs, attitudes, and assumptions about anger have changed, and how that can lead to change in how you handle conflict?

✦ Good people feel anger.

✦ Good people care enough to tell the truth.

✦ Anger identifies problems.

✦ Anger is constructive.

✦ Anger is a good messenger.

✦ Anger can be polite and powerful.

✦ You can be both compassionate and straightforward.

✦ You can be both competent and cooperative.

✦ Conflict helps relationships at home and at work.

✦ You can have consensus and conflict.

✦ You can be cooperative and competitive.

✦ Anger builds strength, clarity, and empowerment for everyone involved.

✦ Anger entails empathy, caring, and compassion.

✦ Conflict is a tool for positive and effective change.

✦ You can be both an authority figure and a caring person.

✦ You can be firm and gentle.

✦ You can be decisive and compassionate.

Do any of these statements sound familiar? Can you think of times you felt angry and behaved in ways that conveyed these beliefs? Did other people seem to feel more comfortable after the interaction? Did your relationships at work or at home improve after conflict was aired and a resolution was achieved?

## Anger Is a Feeling

Healthy anger expressers understand more than just these statements. They know something about feelings that allows them to express themselves with skill, integrity, and genuineness. Healthy anger expressers move into problems as challenges to solve. They do not fear conflict. What are these basic beliefs about feelings that allow healthy anger expressers to develop the emotional awareness, vocabulary, and interpersonal skills to effectively express themselves? Look at this list and see how many of these beliefs about emotions make sense to you now. Have your beliefs changed?

✦ Anger and rage are different.

✦ It is important to name feelings properly and accurately.

✦ Naming feelings leads to expectations and outcomes.

✦ Anger expression leads to a constructive solution to a problem.

✦ Anger is a natural, biological response to a threat. It does not mean you are a bad or undesirable person.

✦ Healthy expression of anger requires integrating both emotional and physical arousal with thinking and purposeful action to arrive at a constructive solution.

✦ Healthy anger expression involves a complex set of developed skills.

✦ Healthy anger expression involves a win-win outcome.

✦ Anger is linked to feeling threatened and is a signal to address the threat.

✦ There are many kinds of threats, and they can be subtle or obvious.

✦ Whether or not you should feel threatened is unimportant. What is important is that you feel threatened.

✦ You feel threatened when something happens that makes you feel hurt, afraid, sad, or vulnerable, and these tender feelings make you want to protect yourself.

✦ Healthy anger expression implies a communication of three basic assumptions: "I respect you. I respect me. And I know that I am aware of a problem between us."

Which of these statements are new to you? Which have always been true, but you've had a hard time putting them into practice? Do you feel that your attitudes, beliefs, and assumptions about anger are changing?

## Anger and Symptoms

Healthy anger expressers do not have the symptoms characteristic of anger avoiders. Healthy anger expressers, more than likely, do not visit their family physician as often, unless they have a chronic medical condition. They do not experience the fatigue and low tolerance levels described in the symptoms of anger avoiders. Healthy anger expressers do not feel the inner tension that accompanies the suppression of feelings. They do not ruminate and obsess about a conflict, thinking over and over what they should have said or wished they had done in the moment.

Healthy anger expressers understand that feelings are natural, healthy, protective, and informative. Feelings are natural in that they are unfiltered responses to an event or interaction. Healthy anger expressers know that your feelings let you know how you are really responding, not how you think you should be responding. Feelings are healthy, meaning there's nothing wrong with having them. Your feelings are simply your feelings about an event. You are not responsible for the feelings you have about an event. But you are responsible for what you do or how you behave with the feelings you have. Healthy anger expressers understand that your feelings are there to protect you by giving you information about when you feel safe and when you don't.

## Anger and Psychological Resources

Because healthy anger expressers do not suppress anger or other feelings as much, they do not deplete their resources. They generally have more energy, feel less burdened by recent interactions, and have more focus to think about or plan for future events. Healthy anger expressers do not become burdened with the conflict of having feelings about feelings. This allows them to have more energy and feel better about themselves. They know that the feelings they have are good to have, and are not ashamed of themselves for having feelings.

Healthy anger expressers live with fewer inner conflicts than anger avoiders. They have less psychological distress, fewer physical illnesses and symptoms, and they exhibit fewer disturbed behaviors. They have more energy available to deal with the various challenges and excitement of living.

## Anger and the Mind in the Body

Because they are less conflicted, healthy anger expressers are more open to feeling what they feel in the moment. This includes physical sensations as well. Healthy anger expressers know their body better because they are open to the sensations and discomforts they feel when they are getting signals that they are reacting to an event or interaction. They know that the fight-or-flight response is natural, and they know how to use this information to calm themselves and deal with the stressor they are experiencing. Healthy anger expressers know how to read their body and know how to calm their body when they are aroused. They know that they must think with a clear mind, not a mind racing with anger, fearful, and full of conflicted thoughts.

Healthy anger expressers understand that very powerful physical sensations are normal and healthy and are not an indication that they are going to lose control. They can feel angry enough to want to yell, scream, or slam their fist into the wall. They can feel fearful enough in a conflict to want to run, give up, or concede defeat. But healthy anger expressers function with these feelings, not without them. They find ways to manage their fears and impulses so that they behave in ways that are goal directed and respectful to all involved. Healthy anger expressers still make mistakes, but they are not ashamed of their mistakes. Instead, they own their mistakes and take responsibility for them.

## Integrating Thoughts and Feelings

Healthy anger expressers know that they must integrate the power of their feelings with the clarity of their thoughts in order to effectively handle conflict and solve problems. They understand that this can be a very difficult process, and that no one can get it right all the time. They build skills and learn from mistakes, and convey this as an accumulated wisdom that helps them in relationships with others. As a result, their relationships tend to be long-term, steady, and deep. Their friends and coworkers know that they will tell the truth, not just what they think others want to hear. They will name uncomfortable crises and conflicts, instead of simply toeing the company line or going along with the crowd. Their sense of safety seems to come from within.

## Healthy Self-Talk

Healthy anger expressers are very active mentally. They are always talking to themselves. They have many helpful phrases that keep them balanced and behaving in line with their values and intentions. They stay alert to interactions and pay attention to their feelings and reactions. As a result, they are seen by others as steady, honest, trustworthy, and principled. They act in accordance with their beliefs, and correct themselves when they stray from themselves. They know they can experience trouble, lose their center, and find it again. Healthy anger expressers can redirect themselves and know how to recognize when they need to do this.

## Anger Expression Is Important

Healthy anger expressers don't have an easy time of things; they just handle things differently. Life may not be easy, but they may feel better about themselves while they are living it. Life is full of difficulties. Some philosophers say it's supposed to be that way. We have much to learn and the difficulties we face give us the opportunities to handle tough times and develop new skills, new perspectives, and find new dimensions and directions in life.

Handling anger and conflict in healthy ways does not in itself lead directly to higher human evolution or new dimensions of consciousness, but it seems that handling anger is necessary to deal with the problems we face every day.

Handling anger takes skill and experience. Developing skill and acquiring experience means that you have to not only accept anger as a necessary part of life but also as an opportunity to grow and expand. Life is full of difficulties. Anger and conflict are opportunities for anger avoiders and anger exploders to learn what healthy anger expressers know, that conflict can be healthy, normal, and helpful.

# Putting It All Together

Chapter 2 introduced a diagram that showed how people may respond to an event with anger or rage:

Event

↓

Perceived threat

↓

Arousal

↓

How you handle that arousal

↓↓

Anger     Rage

An event occurs. That event must have relevance to you; it must be something that threatens your sense of well-being in some way. The threat could be physical, emotional, social, or a variety of other kinds of threats. You have a reaction to that threat. That reaction will at least include a physical response, and may include emotional or intellectual arousal as well. You may find yourself breathing more rapidly; you may find that your thoughts are racing and your emotions may be cycling though patterns of fear, anger, doubt, uncertainty, and other emotions.

Healthy anger expressers recognize these signs of arousal and begin to employ the ideas and techniques described in this book. They slow down their breathing and regulate their sympathetic nervous system. They regain control of the mind in their body, without forgetting that there is a problem to solve. They begin to use self-talk both to calm themselves and to redirect their efforts toward a constructive goal.

Healthy anger expressers then choose an angry response; they do not choose a rageful response. They have a clear idea about what the problem is and how they want to respond. They keep their value system intact and do not behave before they think. Instead of regretting what they did, healthy anger expressers continue to be present, working toward a healthy solution and adjusting their approach as the situation changes. Their choice of an angry approach over a rageful one reflects a respect for themselves, as well as for the person they are interacting with. When it's all over, healthy anger expressers can easily shake hands, forgive, and move on, or otherwise finish the interaction and not carry the residual feelings around with them. Since they do not employ rageful responses, there is not a destructive outcome to spoil future interactions.

# Integrating Anger Responses

Healthy anger expression can be challenging, and it requires both skills and experience. But it also provides opportunities to grow in new ways. Conflict can provide the need to change basic limitations we harbor about ourselves. These limitations can be difficult to overcome, even in the best of circumstances.

The situations anger avoiders face are primarily, but not exclusively, in personal relationships and workplace relationships. The following vignette illustrates the complexity involved in beginning the healthy expression of anger where anger had been previously assumed to be dangerous and uncomfortable. As you will see, breaking an established pattern can feel like a betrayal and can be very threatening to the partner as well as to the relationship itself.

### ✦ Al and Cindy

Al and Cindy had been married for four years, after dating for nearly two years. They had a passionate courtship filled with romance, trips, new careers, and excitement. After their wedding, their marriage seemed to cool, however. Al in particular appeared to lose his zest.

He didn't care where they were when they went out, always deferring to her wishes, saying "I don't care honey, you choose." He slept later and seemed generally unexcited. When Cindy complained about his lack of direction or clarity in how he wanted to spend time with her, Al seemed to sink even more into a growing apathy. He wasn't particularly excited about his job and lost interest in his usual activities except for golf, which Cindy felt only served the purpose of taking him away from her for extended periods of time. Cindy complained more often. Al withdrew more. They saw a marriage therapist, but it didn't help. Al didn't have the energy to face the problem in the marriage. So he was referred for individual therapy.

In therapy, Al did not appear to be depressed. He had a boyish energy about him. His mood and affect were normal. He functioned more than adequately at work and exercised on a regular basis. He slept well and did not suffer from undue low self-esteem. Al knew that he was the problem in the marriage and was in therapy "to be fixed." He said he didn't know what the problem was and didn't know what to do to make it better.

Upon closer study, Al fit the pattern of being an anger avoider. He had numerous conflicts with his father, who was intrusive and controlling. Al felt angered by his father's pattern of belittling Al. Al also described similar patterns with his wife. When she first complained about Al's behavior—how he didn't hang up his coat, let junk mail pile up in the kitchen, and didn't do his share of the dishes—Al fought back and defended himself. He'd say he was tired, or didn't notice, or wanted to clean up later. Cindy would become more insistent and would not back down from her complaint, so Al would back down. When Al saw that she would fight back, he quit, just like he did with his father. But as he fell silent more and more, he also appeared apathetic and didn't display much interest in Cindy. He still loved her though, and was motivated to change in order to save his marriage.

Al didn't avoid anger because he feared conflict or because he feared he'd explode. He simply didn't know what to do, for he never learned healthy anger expression skills. He found it easier to avoid his feelings than to be uncomfortable. He had developed a way to "just let it go" and not carry around any tension or discomfort. In therapy, Al focused on learning how to express his anger. Like a lot of anger avoiders, he first had to learn to pay attention to his body's reaction to conflict. Al seemed to be comforted with a structured approach to healthy anger expression.

One night, Al and Cindy went out to dinner at a restaurant that Al had chosen for a change. During dinner Cindy started to tell Al about the rotten day she had had. Then it seemed to Al that she turned her anger on him. She started complaining about Al's work schedule and a golfing trip he had planned months ago. She started to mention something else, but Al cut her off with a blunt, "Hey, don't take your bad day out on me!" Cindy was startled and paused to take in the sudden change in Al's behavior. Usually he would just sit, listen, and look blank. Now Cindy didn't quite know what to do. She started to talk again about something he was doing, but Al cut her off. "It's not my fault you had a rough day."

Cindy didn't like this. She reasserted herself and told him not to talk to her that way. Al said, "Hey, what did I do?" There was a long, pregnant pause between them. Al was feeling very uncomfortable and was squirming on the inside. But he just looked at her, trying not to blink.

After what seemed like an eternity, Al remembered some of the skills he had learned in therapy. He took a deep breath and shook himself out of what seemed like a rigid, statuelike stance. He softly said, "I know that was new for you; it was new for me too. But I was uncomfortable with the way I felt when you started talking to me. I want to listen to you, but I need you to listen to me too."

Cindy looked at the new Al. He seemed both old and familiar and new and uncertain to her right now. Their relationship was strained now, not by the anger they had avoided, but by the anger Al introduced into the relationship for a change. Cindy finally said, "Okay, I hear you. I'm sorry I took my day out on you." Al didn't really know what to say now. He didn't feel like he had won, but for a change he didn't feel like he had lost either. Finally he recovered enough to simply say, "Thanks."

Al and Cindy faced a new experience when Al began the process of changing his behavior and directly facing conflict instead of avoiding or denying it. Neither knew what to do. There was a new stress in their relationship. Now they had the opportunity to deal with each other in an honest, intimate, problem-solving way.

Change brings stress. You might think that changing troubled patterns brings relief. It does, but the initial experiences can be unstable and uncoordinated. This makes sense when you consider that healthy anger expression is a learned skill. It's like any new task, such as skiing, Ping-Pong, or learning a new language or other new ways of moving, thinking, or speaking; you're not necessarily good at it at first. It takes practice to get past the initial experiences of feeling awkward, uncertain, and doubtful about your ability to master this new skill. Learning healthy patterns of anger expression is the same. As Al and Cindy found, beginning the process of change can initially bring a level of discomfort that can almost make you want to go back to your old patterns.

But expression of anger doesn't always happen in standard relationships and expected interactions. Sometimes you're on your own.

### ✦ Billy's Story

Billy was driving back from the shopping center with his family. Because of recent construction, the bridge was more difficult to navigate than usual. Billy was in the left lane, with cars coming toward him from the other direction, while a large pickup truck was on his right. When the truck driver crossed the dotted line to avoid running into the side of the bridge, he entered Billy's lane. Billy laid on the horn, and the startled truck driver overcorrected and nearly hit the side of the bridge.

Once they were off the bridge, the driver started shouting and gesturing at Billy. This went on for a mile, until they came to a light where Billy was turning left. The truck driver came up on Billy's right and stared at Billy. Billy looked back at the truck driver. Billy knew what was going on. He knew that they'd look at each other until one of them made a move.

Then both would get out of their vehicles, and no telling what would happen.

Billy was angry too. The guy hadn't paid attention and had almost forced him into oncoming traffic. Billy had played football in high school and was known for not backing down from a fight. But Billy was with his wife and two daughters. Fighting was not an a option. So he took a long breath. Then he said to himself what he knew he couldn't say to the other guy: "You didn't notice that you were pushing me over into oncoming traffic. You were startled and jolted when I blew the horn, and that nearly threw you into the side of the bridge. I was as scared as you at that moment. We will just have to let it go. You didn't mean to ride me over the line, and I didn't mean to scare you." Then Billy looked away. Out of the corner of his eye, he noticed the other driver did the same after another minute.

Billy had to handle this conflict by himself. Both men clearly felt threatened and started to react aggressively. But Billy was able to do something to solve the problem. He couldn't rely on the other guy to talk it out or to see the event from his perspective, so he had to solve the problem with the resources he had available to him.

Unlike this scenario, however, most events occur in ongoing relationships: in our relationships at home or at work. When you have ongoing contact with someone, changing your behavior can be both more difficult and more meaningful. Sometimes it takes both parties to solve the problem.

### ✦ Mary's Story

Mary said she would be home by 6 P.M. John planned the evening accordingly. When she finally walked in the door at 9:15, John was angry. It's easy to see why. He had taken care of the kids, dinner, homework, and the bedtime routine by himself. But that wasn't all. John also had many unnamed fears and threats that were fueling his anger. John feared that Mary might have been out with someone else, threatening his sense of well-being in the relationship. She might have been out with her

girlfriends, taking advantage of John's easy nature.
She could have just blown off the entire evening and
indulged herself in a shopping trip without bothering to
even tell John. The two latter scenarios would have left
him feeling foolish, taken for granted, and unappreciated.
John's anger was fueled by his fears and by the fact that
he felt threatened.

By the time Mary got home, John was all worked
up. "Where were you?" he demanded. Mary now felt
attacked and threatened, and felt her own anger. "There
was an accident, and the highway was a parking lot.
I couldn't get to a phone to call you," she nearly shouted
back at him.

Now John felt embarrassed and guilty for creating
all of the scenarios that had fed his anger. But he hadn't
quite calmed down from his fury yet. He paused, took a
breath, held his gaze on Mary's face, but straightened and
softened his body. "Oh!" he said. Then, after a few
seconds, he offered, "I didn't know that. I was worried
sick. I'm sorry I attacked you like that." Mary felt the
softening of John's stance, but she dealt with her feelings
first. "Yes, that really hurt when you jumped on me as
soon as I came in. I was really upset about being late,
and I wasn't expecting you to attack me." John struggled
with the guilt that had replaced his anger. "I'm sorry," he
said simply. Mary was slower to soften. "I understand
you were worried and probably tired after taking care of
everything, but that's no way to greet me. It's like you
didn't trust that I was delayed for a good reason."

John felt the urge to protect and defend himself.
After all, here he was at home, taking care of the kids
and the house chores while Mary was late, and now he
was the one feeling guilty! He wanted to blurt out
"Gimme a break!" but instead took a calm breath and
reached his hand out to her. "I know that was unfair to
you. You didn't deserve that. I'm sorry." Mary took his
hand. "Thanks. Was it a hard night?"

It took both Mary and John to stay focused on their problem
as it evolved. Both thought they were in the right and felt hurt by
the other's response. Both had to be honest about their feelings to
themselves and to their partner.

# Changing Your Beliefs and Behaviors

Take out your journal again. Make a list of the ideas in this chapter that struck you as important. Which ones were new? Which ones did you recognize from earlier chapters? Which ideas will you have an easier time putting into practice now?

Write out your three-step assignment.

1. What happened to make you learn to feel afraid of expressing your anger?

2. How has that limited and harmed your life so far?

3. What will you do now that you are back in charge of your life?

# 8

# women and anger avoidance: relationship dilemmas

This chapter and the following chapter are devoted to building an awareness of how anger can bring different conflicts for men and women. This chapter is on women and the unique difficulties they face expressing anger in relationships at work or at home. The goal is to raise a general awareness of and appreciation for the difficulties women may face as they learn to express anger in healthy ways. Understanding gender differences in relation to expressing anger can help in the change process and lead to more effective outcomes.

Chris Kilmartin wrote the next chapter on men and anger avoidance. Chris is a good friend and an esteemed colleague. He and I cowrote a book on men's issues (Lynch and Kilmartin 1999). He is an expert on men and masculinity so I am sure you will find his discussion of men and anger interesting and informative. Chris's chapter will introduce you to the contributions that the field of men's studies brings to the understanding of men and masculinity. Because men frequently have a smaller emotional vocabulary and diminished awareness of feelings, Chris' chapter will introduce you to why and how men lose awareness of feelings and why it is so important that men be reintroduced to this vocabulary. Again, knowing what you are feeling, naming it properly, and having a full range of options is vital to healthy expression of anger. While men misname anger for different reasons than do women, they need the same skills and orientation to anger as women do.

Chris and I share many views on gender. We both prefer to use the terms masculinity and femininity when referring to styles of functioning in the world. We use these terms instead of male and female for very important reasons. Those reasons are worth exploring before I get into this chapter.

# Femininity and Masculinity

We all have masculine and feminine traits, and each of us has our own unique combination of these traits. Masculinity is associated with assertiveness, getting the job done, responsibility for self, and competing for dominance. Femininity is associated with maintaining group cohesion, serving the needs of the family, friends, or community, and being loyal in and to relationships. Any given man could have masculine traits and, at the same time, have feminine traits. Similarly, any given woman has both masculine and feminine traits, and how these traits blend in her overall makeup adds to her personality and her uniqueness. The emphasis of this chapter will be on femininity and the difficulties it brings into a healthy expression of anger. However, while this chapter will focus on women, it is very possible that a woman reader will feel more connection with the discussion in chapter 9. Likewise, and man might feel that this chapter describes his experience better than the chapter on men does. That's okay. The terms *masculinity* and *femininity* are used here for that very reason, to avoid generalizing about men and women.

Given those qualifiers, this chapter will focus on the unique experiences and difficulties that women face when dealing with interpersonal expressions of anger and conflict. While there are many aspects of women's identity, the development of femininity, and the experiences that girls and women face, this chapter focuses only on those traits that are related to having difficulty with the expression of anger and conflict. The text and the stories will focus on generalized expectations that apply to a feminine way of being and result in a limitation or restriction of a full range of emotional expression.

# Autonomous Self and Relational Self

One way to greatly simplify a description of personality and functioning in the world is to say that we are composed of our autonomous self and our relational self. The *autonomous self* is that part in each of us that defines each of us as unique. The autonomous self is represented by the "I" in your identity. The autonomous self is usually associated with the masculine part of a person's identity. The relational self is that part of a person that is connected to family, community, friends, or other relationships. It is the "we" in your identity. The *relational self* is usually associated with the feminine part of your identity. People all have aspects of both autonomous and relational functioning, and identity is comprised of both of these characteristics or tendencies. After all, no one lives in total isolation or total immersion in a group. We are both individuals and members of a community.

We are defined as much by our relationships and how we conduct and nurture these relationships as we are by what we do and accomplish as individuals. If you only based your identity on your autonomous self, you would accomplish a lot, strive for new challenges, and conquer many goals. But you would live either in isolation from others or at war with others, always competing to maintain your individuality or to ensure your survival, regardless of the outcome that others experience. If you only based your identity on your relational self, you would be well connected to everyone around you and would serve the community's needs. But you would lose a sense of who you are, what your life is about, and what you bring as your unique contribution to the world.

Both your relational and your autonomous self are vital to your overall identity and your ability to function in the world. You would be limited without either one of these identities. Neither is inherently better. They are different. Together they add, in different measures, to your identity. You can be, and certainly need to be, more masculine in one situation and more feminine in another, or more autonomous in one situation and more relational in another, depending on the needs and demands of the situation. The more flexible you are, and the more you are able to adapt to different situations, the better you can apply yourself to the events and interactions you experience.

# Women and the Relational Self

More so than men, women tend to develop the relational self, at times to the detriment of the autonomous self. More so than women, men tend to develop the autonomous self, sometimes to the detriment of the relational self. Through this way of looking at men and women, you can understand some of the standard gender differences. In families, men are frequently criticized by their wives for "not getting it." Women say, "I feel like I have another kid to take care of. He's only interested in what he's interested in, and it doesn't include me or the kids." She is describing him from a relational perspective. From her point of view, he can appear to be self-centered and self-serving. Men, on the other hand, complain that she "wants to take over everything I do. She wants us to go everywhere together and always wants to talk about stuff. I just want to be left alone sometimes." He is describing her from an autonomous point of view. To him, she can look like she wants to engulf him and take over his life.

But neither of these two ways of being in the world is better than the other. They are simply different. She wants to connect with him because she has developed her relational self, possibly to the detriment of her autonomous self. He wants space and distance because he has developed his autonomous self, possibly to the detriment of his relational self. Each person finds the other threatening, yet each wants the relationship to work. Some theories of marriage speculate that people marry to somehow find their own missing parts. Men marry women, in part, to learn how to be relational without losing autonomy. Women marry men, according to this theory, to find their autonomous self.

But the differences between these ways of being in the world get in the way of communication and complicate the relationship. Both men and women fear losing the self they have to the self they are seeking to find in order to complete themselves. Both defend their established self and seek to change their partner instead. Men say, "If only women were more like men." Women say, "I chase him around just to get him to pay attention to me and spend some time with me." Each wants the other to change to the way of being that is known and safe, whether it is relational or autonomous.

# The Relational Self and Femininity

According to this way of looking at the genders, women find meaning and importance in relationships. In relationships women find companionship and comfort, meaning and purpose, and a way of serving something greater than themselves. Some argue that the socialization process, or how we learn how we are supposed to behave, shapes girls to be more aware of feelings and connections to others. Girls are socialized to be cooperative, whereas boys are socialized to be competitive or aggressive. Over time, this can have an effect that significantly shapes how girls, and women, experience themselves in the world and when they are being successful in their attempts to form a feminine identity. The behaviors that are rewarded might be described as relationship focused rather than individual achievement focused. Although these patterns may be changing, there are still large differences in the ways that boys and girls are socialized.

Girls find that they fit gender role expectations, that is, they behave the way they are supposed to behave, when they form a strong relational self. In adolescence, this may be by learning to be a good listener, sharing feelings and excitement with girlfriends, paying attention to how friends are feeling, and giving extra attention when a friend is feeling down. As a woman, this can be manifested by serving the needs of a family, maintaining a good workplace environment, or helping to make the schools a safer and better place to learn. A relational way of being in the world reflects loyalty, commitment to a cause greater than yourself, and being aware of how your actions make others feel and what makes others feel happy and cared for.

A relational way of being in the world frequently means saying "yes" more than saying "no." "Yes" is said in response to requests that require time, effort, and some kind of sacrifice. "Yes" keeps relational connections open. "Yes" implies more open personal boundaries, as opposed to "no," which implies clear boundaries and a difference between the needs of the self and the needs of others. In a manner of speaking, girls learn "yes" where boys learn "no." The relational self combines one's own needs with the needs of the group. Too often this leads to women who experience themselves as chronically depressed, guilty, or full of self-doubt when they exert their independence or otherwise break the rules and act in ways that assert their autonomy. It is no wonder that the diagnosis of *codependence*, a condition characterized by losing your identity in your ability to make others at ease, was first introduced in the treatment of women. Relational functioning is vital to a balanced identity, but, like many things, it can get out of balance and wreak havoc. While a relational way of being in the world is vital to the cohesion of our families and is the fabric of our culture, it can take a tremendous toll on the individual when overdeveloped to the exclusion of the autonomous self.

# Femininity and Development

Relational identity takes a toll on development. This toll is reflected in the assumption that girls will be more cooperative and attentive to feelings than boys. This pattern in childhood leads to predictable and parallel patterns in adults. This next section will discuss general gender assumptions and expectations and the predictable outcomes in adult patterns of interaction that are gender based.

## Role Development

Girls (and women) learn important cultural expectations of feminity. They learn that appearances matter. How you look, or how you appear to be, tells people a lot about you. Generally speaking, women are valued for attractiveness, pleasantness, and the ability to provide emotional nurturance. When they comply with these expectations, women are rewarded not for being who they are, but for looking to others and behaving toward others like they are supposed to behave. The emphasis here is not on how you develop individuality, but rather on how you meet group or cultural expectations. Girls, as a group, learn to be caring and sensitive to the feelings of others.

Indeed, in most families it is the mother who provides emotional nurturance, even though fathers are just as capable of developing these skills. Girls learn that what they do is not as important as what boys do. Boys get more attention in school, whether they behave or misbehave. Girls learn to defer, to take care of the needs and feelings of others, to be polite, to be emotional and sensitive, gentle and tactful, and to be home oriented and neat.

All of this is not to say that all girls are the same, any more than all boys are the same. But general social expectations shape girls' development, and because of these expectations, girls experience certain limitations that influence who they can become and how they can behave. Many of these patterns are clearly changing for a new generation of girls, but many women grew up with these traditional, stereotyped expectations.

Early expectations exert a profound influence on women's behavior. When we look at the differences in social expectations of adult men and women, we see how early development leaves men and women with limited roles. Men are supposed to be strong, hide their feelings, act in a traditional manly way, be aggressive, and look muscular. Women are supposed to look attractive and feminine, and be smart, sensitive, and emotional. These are limiting roles for men and women. Women may feel confined by these limitations. There are many behaviors that women are not supposed to exhibit but need to utilize in order to function and survive in this world. Women may face many prohibitions and restrictions that men do not face. For instance, women are not supposed to be independent; men are. Women are not supposed to be aggressive; men are. Women are not supposed to be outspoken; men are. Women are not supposed to take a stand; men are. Women are supposed to be emotional, considerate, kind, and understanding. In reality, few men fit the profile of traditional masculinity, and few women want the limitations imposed by traditional ideas of femininity. Yet, because these expectations are subtle and pervasive when you learn how to be a boy or a girl, you may be to some extent defined by how well you conform to these expectations.

## Adult Development

A woman's identity, based on feminine principles or concepts, can set her up for limited adult functioning, especially in the area of expression of anger and conflict. Expressing these feelings becomes difficult for women because the roles ascribed to women do not freely and easily allow for conflict and disagreement, which tend to be seen as requiring masculine traits. Women who are supposed to be feminine but who have masculine traits may experience unique and difficult interactions. In the terms used before, women's relational functioning, or their attention to the needs of their relationships, can clash with their autonomous needs, or their needs to assert their individuality. In these situations women may have few viable and healthy options for handling conflict or expressing anger. When women are limited, by themselves or by cultural expectations, we all suffer. Work productivity decreases or at least does not benefit from new and fresh ideas, home relationships are limited and therefore less satisfying, and our culture loses out on great ideas and innovations. Femininity plays a pervasive role in the development of women. While there is much that is changing in how women are treated, much remains the same. Women still face personal and professional dangers when they break gender roles and freely express anger and conflict or otherwise behave in ways that are not traditionally feminine.

From this perspective on some of the developmental forces that shape how women "should" behave and handle themselves in relationships, predictable problems occur when conflict arises. In personal areas, women may experience difficulties expressing anger because of fears that they

✦ will harm the relationship that they are in and in which they are experiencing anger

✦ will feel bad about themselves, as if they have broken some unspoken rule about how women should behave

✦ will feel they are responsible for the feelings others have as a result of the anger they express

✦ will face real possibilities that they will be beaten or otherwise harmed if they break the rules and express conflict in an intimate relationship

## ✦ Beverly's Story

Beverly and Mike had what's referred to as a traditional arrangement. He worked outside the home, and she was a homemaker. She took care of the kids, the schedules, the shopping, and the bumps and scrapes, physical and psychological, that are part of daily family life with three kids. Mike "pulled the barge" by himself and provided for the family's needs by throwing himself into his work. After a few years, their relationship and patterns had become standard. Beverly took care of the kids and Mike, and was the peacemaker to his temper, which had grown more abrasive and troublesome as his work stress increased and his ability to relax and join the family fun decreased. Beverly frequently translated Mike to the kids, "Your father is tired," or, "He loves you, but he has a lot of responsibilities." Or, "He didn't mean that. You have to see all that he does for you." Beverly excused his absences, forgave his outbursts, and understood his frustrations. Beverly took care of Mike in noticeable and obvious ways. In less obvious ways, at least not so noticeable to Mike, he grew more and more dependent on her. His friendships fell to the wayside. He relied on her friendship for social contact. He didn't know the kids as well as she did, and seemed to always do or say the wrong thing. He felt alone and lonely, as men frequently do. And as often happens, Beverly understood what was happening to Mike and what was going on between the two of them while Mike didn't. Somehow Mike had grown used to not being fully responsible for his behavior in the home. Beverly always seemed to make it all better and smooth things over.

One day, Mike had had an unusually stressful day at work. At least that's what he said to himself. Five minutes after getting home, he called their youngest son lazy and sloppy because he had left the family room a mess. Mike didn't stop there. He went on to call his son ungrateful and spoiled. Mike was escalating, didn't notice it, and did nothing to stop. He said he was disgusted with his son and told him that he wasn't worth the effort. Mike's son was devastated by this verbal battering. He broke down in tears and ran to Beverly. Mike let loose with one last shot, "Sure, now go run to your mother!"

Beverly did something different. Perhaps she had read a book on the healthy expression of anger, or maybe she was beginning to feel that there was something unhealthy in this family psychological air. Who knows why she did what she did? But instead of making it all better and telling her son that his father just had a hard day and didn't mean it, she said to Mike, "I know you're tired and worn-out. But you've really hurt your son's feelings. That was totally uncalled for. Take a look at your son. Look at how you've made him feel. That's how you make all of us feel when you do that." Beverly named what Mike did and didn't clean up his mess.

She continued, "I don't like this. You come home and take your mood out on the kids and I'm supposed to understand you and the kids, and fix both of you. I didn't sign up for this. Something has to change. I'm not going to continue to live this way."

Beverly couldn't believe what had come out of her mouth. She had never spoken up before and was nervous about what would happen next. She knew she hadn't done anything wrong but wasn't real sure of herself.

Mike didn't know what to do or say either. This had never happened before. He said, "What are you saying? Didn't sign up for what? Not going to live what way?" Mike was quite frightened. He felt very threatened by Beverly's stance. He relied on her for everything. He suddenly felt empty inside and had trouble breathing. He really felt ashamed of what he did and wanted her to make it better. But in typical male fashion, he became outraged in order to protect himself. He couldn't ask for what he really needed and talk with his partner about the troubles he felt, or admit to and correct his behavior. He tried to reestablish his authority instead.

"Well, if that's the way you feel," he said and walked out. He didn't know what else to say and didn't want to stand there and say nothing. Doing so would have left him feeling too exposed and vulnerable. So he walked out of the room. Beverly knew she had done nothing wrong, but she wondered. "Did I say the right thing? Was I too abrupt? Should I have been more understanding?" The tension remained in the house for several days, and they seemed to move past it when they went to an extended family gathering and everyone marveled at how nicely their kids behaved.

Beverly responded in a healthy manner. She named a problem and held Mike accountable without shaming him or blasting him in return. Mike was too threatened to respond, however. When she expressed her anger at Mike's behavior, as mildly as she did, her actions changed, and therefore threatened the relationships that she was keeping stable. When Mike left the room, she backed off. Again, Beverly felt responsible for holding the family together. After all, that was their bargain. It was her job to keep the home life intact and keep everyone together.

## ✦ Laura's Story

Laura was independent and stable. She enjoyed her career and her social life. She had a nice apartment, traveled and vacationed comfortably, and shared life with a few well-chosen and well-nurtured friends. She started dating Jed a few months back. They had similar interests, and hiked, biked, and explored the outdoors together. This was the first real dating she had done in years, since the breakup with her fiancé of three years. She liked dating again, and was happy to be with such a goodlooking, nice guy. They enjoyed each other's company.

At first, Laura thought Jed was a real man's man. He was a little on the macho side and lived a man's lifestyle, with a poor diet and frequent injuries from pushing the limits of whatever he was doing. But Laura quickly began to understand that behind the bravado and macho front was a good bit of insecurity. He got upset too quickly over little things that went wrong and had a hard time calming down when he did get upset.

Once, at a dinner gathering, Jed seemed to be invested in maintaining a man's man image and didn't pay much attention to Laura. He told guy stories and talked over her when she tried to start her own conversation. She was uncomfortable with this behavior and told him so on the way home. She told him she didn't like how he treated her and asked him why he did that.

Up to this point, their relationship had been without confrontation or conflict. Laura's confrontation hit Jed's insecurity. He had not been challenged like this before. He was used to getting his way and being the life of the party. Jed had lots of funny stories to tell and told them well. He played to a crowd with ease and seemed to gather energy as other people laughed at his stories. But here he was, being confronted with the effect of his behavior. Jed looked at Laura, and in the usual masculine initial response, asked, "What do you mean?" Laura didn't budge and said, "You know what I mean. You didn't talk to me, or let anyone else talk most of the evening. I felt embarrassed after a while. These are my friends. I don't like being shut out of the conversation like that or ignored by the person I'm with." Jed kept up the innocence, "I didn't ignore you!" Laura paused, saw the endless argument ahead and said, "I don't like this. This is a problem. I need something else from you when we're out with other people."

Both stopped and just looked at each other. Their easy relationship had changed. Both knew it. The rules of the relationship no longer fit stereotyped roles. This interaction was new and uncomfortable. What would happen next? Could their relationship, which both had valued, survive this challenge? Would Jed feel threatened and refuse to acknowledge his role in this? Would Laura take care of him in order to save the relationship or let him figure it out for himself? Would the relationship evolve or end? Laura wondered deep within herself if she had done the right thing. She knew that Jed had insecurities. Had she spoken too strongly? Should she have tolerated the problem for now? Was standing up for herself right then worth losing this relationship?

As with many couples, Laura had more relationship skills and awareness than Jed did. So her decision to confront him about his behavior and effect this had on him threatened the relationship. He did not have the personal comfort and wherewithal to simply and nondefensively respond, "Wow! I'm sorry. I was having such a good time I forgot all about you. That must have felt terrible for you. I need to pay attention when I get revved up. It's fun to have fun, but I don't need to leave you out like that." Laura knew Jed would have trouble handling this confrontation and that he might react defensively. She understood that he might have trouble handling conflict in a relationship. But she doubted herself too. She feared that she had made him feel bad and may have stressed a good relationship.

Like Beverly, Laura doubted herself. Her relational functioning was a stronger and more grounded part of her identity. She was socialized to take care of the relationship. When she faced the dilemma of taking care of the relationship or taking care of herself, she naturally doubted herself.

### ✦ *Marina's Story*

Marina was in what some people call a midlife crisis. Her kids were still pretty young, and she didn't like feeling locked into a limited life of diapers and baths. She loved her husband, Kevin, but felt a sense of dissatisfaction in her life. She wasn't looking for someone else; she just wanted more out of this life. They had stable careers, many friends, and long years together raising the kids. The problem was that the relationship didn't work for Marina anymore, and she hadn't thought she would feel this way about raising a family or being married.

Kevin assumed a lot of male privilege. He'd have a night out with the guys and feel free to do whatever the guys were doing. Marina was tolerant of the bars he went to and the shenanigans "the boys" got away with. But Marina wasn't free to do the same. She had female friends, but felt her time with them was limited by Kevin's time out of the house or by his need to have her home when he was home. There was lots of "guy time" but little to no "girl time." Marina felt more resentful and didn't like sacrificing her needs for his on such a regular basis.

She scheduled a night out with the girls, even offered to get a sitter, and had everything planned. The girls were going bowling and then over to a friend's house for chips and a card game. Kevin made fun of it all at first. But when he saw that she was serious, he became more rigid and demanding. Secretly, Kevin feared what many men fear when their wives go out for the evening. They fear she'll find something better and not come back. Men often can't talk about their relationship insecurities, so frequently they try to control their wives instead, in order to feel safe. Kevin also wondered if the guys would think poorly of him and give him a rough time if they found out that he had stayed home and taken care of dinner and diapers while his wife went out with the girls. Kevin felt threatened by Marina's plans.

When ridicule didn't work he became more dominant. "No you're not!" he shouted. "Yes I am!" she replied. "I've washed your clothes, cooked your dinners, taken care of your kids, and now I'm going out with my friends, and you're going to take care of the kids." Kevin lied. "I'm going out; I've got plans with the guys." Marina responded, "Then you get a sitter." Kevin felt threatened, out of control, and powerless. But Marina didn't back down.

The tension escalated. Marina moved toward the door and Kevin hit her. Marina stepped back and looked right at him. "That's the last time that will happen," she said and called the police. Kevin was charged with domestic violence. Marina won the battle but felt anything but victorious. When she talked to her girlfriends, they supported her, but she couldn't shake the feeling that she had done something wrong and had changed her family life forever.

Hopefully, Marina did change her family life. Hopefully, Kevin was court ordered into a domestic violence treatment program, learned about the power and control he felt he needed and held over Marina's life, looked at the imbalance in the relationship, and learned how to be a better husband and partner to Marina. Marina didn't do anything wrong. In fact, she did everything correctly. But because she'd broken out of her role, she felt awful. Like Beverly and Laura, Marina felt unsure of herself when she took care of herself before she took care of the relationship. It was easier for her to feel guilt and regret than it was for her to feel sure of herself. It was easier to feel compassion for Kevin's plight with the police than it was for her to feel compassion for herself and what this lifestyle was costing her.

## ✦ Carol's Story

Carol and Wendy were frequently at the same social gatherings. They liked each other and had mutual friends and interests. This was the spring semester of their senior year in high school and both were enjoying the parties and looking forward to their upcoming graduation. Carol and Wendy had done well throughout their school careers. Carol planned to attend college next year. Wendy wanted to work and travel first.

At a pregraduation party attended by kids from several nearby high schools, both met Daren. He was handsome but quiet and unassuming. He seemed slightly awkward, like he was alone and out of his comfort zone. Daren had come with a couple of guys, but they were more gregarious and had gone off with a different crowd at the party, leaving Daren by himself. Both Carol and Wendy saw him, liked what they saw, and started talking with him. After a while, Daren seemed to like Carol more. He smiled more when talking with her and loosened up enough to enjoy himself. Wendy was oblivious to this, but Carol and Daren weren't. They had a little thing going.

Suddenly, in the middle of Daren's talk with Carol, Wendy jumped up and said to Daren, "Hey! That's my favorite song, come dance with me!" Carol felt suddenly aroused, alarmed, and flooded with feelings. She wanted to say, "Don't, I'm talking with him," but she didn't. Carol lowered her eyes. Daren was confused. He looked from Wendy to Carol and back at Wendy again. Carol took a step back. Carol didn't want to embarrass Wendy or make Wendy feel foolish. She wondered what Wendy's friends would think of her if Carol stopped Wendy from dancing with Daren, and what stories would circulate about her.

Carol knew Daren was socially shy and felt uncomfortable in this awkward moment. She could sense he was unsure of himself and did not know what to do either. Suddenly she said, "Look! There's Margaret!" and went off to join another group of kids. Carol had an empty feeling in the pit of her stomach for the rest of the evening.

Carol was aware of everyone's feelings and the difficulties everyone experienced. She didn't want to be seen by others as pushy or as someone who would steal a boyfriend. Carol couldn't find a way to be assertive without being selfish, so she abandoned her own needs and feelings, and avoided the conflict. Carol was a "good girl."

## In the Workplace

In professional settings, women often face subtle or overt rejection when they acknowledge conflict or openly voice their differences. Specifically, women face

+ potential loss of a job or the connections and networking that are frequently necessary for a successful career

+ feeling or actually being ostracized, labeled in very negative terms, and punished in relationships by being snubbed by coworkers for not playing by the rules

## ✦ Fran's Story

Fran and Rachel were part of a crew of six women who constituted the shipping and receiving office in a small business. Fran was older by a half generation, but everyone worked together and got along. Fran was known as a hard worker. Her old-timer work ethic was evident. She never made personal calls on company time and never left work early. She was diligent, thorough, and conscientious. Every employer would like to have a room full of Frans. Efficiency and productivity would soar.

Rachel and the others were all young mothers or single women. They had active social or family lives and had a lot of personal business to attend to on a daily basis. Fran didn't like this, but she found ways to tolerate their chatter about their personal lives. She tolerated their less-efficient and less-focused work habits. Fran had worked with younger people before, and though she thought poorly about changing work ethics in the younger generation, she found ways to stay focused on her work and ignore these differences.

For three days running, Rachel had phoned ahead to tell Fran that she'd be a few minutes late to work. They worked as a team and let each other know when they were coming or going. Fran didn't say anything about this, but she had strong feelings about Rachel's tardy behavior. On the third day, their supervisor walked by and asked where Rachel was. Fran pretended not to hear, but the supervisor repeated the question. Fran found herself lying, "I don't know, she's around here somewhere." Fran couldn't believe what she had just done. She had never told a lie like that before. Fran didn't like conflict and stayed focused on her work, in part to avoid this kind of stuff. She was mad at herself, but when Rachel came in to work, Fran didn't look up from her desk to greet Rachel. When Rachel got settled at her station, Fran said, again without looking up and acknowledging Rachel, "I won't cover for you anymore. The next time you're late, you will have to say where you were."

Rachel heard Fran's words and the style Fran used to communicate and felt surprisingly insulted. Rachel didn't respond, but by lunchtime everyone knew what Fran had said. The other workers avoided Fran and were cool and businesslike when they had to communicate with her. Fran got the message. She had broken ranks. In the "us versus them" world she had become a "them." Even though Fran had never fully joined the crowd, she had never been excluded either. A week later, Fran submitted her resignation. Her supervisor was stunned and offered to help solve any problem that bothered Fran. But Fran was characteristically tight-lipped and simply said it was time for her to move on.

Fran wanted to avoid anger but couldn't. She tried to avoid problems in her interaction with the supervisor but violated her autonomy in doing so by telling a lie. To recover from that interaction, she confronted Rachel. But she suffered the consequences by being ostracized by everyone. Her behavior separated her from her coworkers, and they reacted to the relational impact of her words.

Sometimes women face catastrophic consequences at work when they don't "act like a woman." Here is a true story that demonstrates the consequences that can occur when women break the expected rules of behavior:

A woman came up for review for partnership in a major accounting firm. She had brought in more business and income to the company than any of the other people up for partnership. Yet she was denied the promotion and the opportunity for partnership. The reason given for denying her the partnership status and rewards she had earned was that she displayed "interpersonal skills problems." But the nature of these problems would be corrected if she walked, talked, and dressed more femininely. One of her detractors suggested she go to "charm school." Would this have happened to a man? Would a man be denied promotion if he was as successful and had the same "interpersonal skills problems"? (Crawford and Unger 1996, 133).

# Changing Your Beliefs and Behaviors

Take out your journal again. What ideas in this chapter were new? What ideas were stimulated or renewed by what you've read? What differences do you think women face in the healthy expression of anger and management of conflict? What difficulties do you think both men and women face?

Now write out your three-step exercise.

1. What did you learn about being you, male or female, that has limited your expression of anger because of concern and guilt about how you would make others feel?

2. How has this limited your life so far?

3. What will you do now that you are getting control of your life?

# 9

# men, anger, and rage

## By Christopher Kilmartin

Anger is an emotion that many people identify with men. Some men have a good deal of difficulty in even identifying most of their feelings, but they have no problem knowing when they are angry, since our culture expects men to be angry and validates that feeling. At the same time, the culture invalidates many other feelings (such as sadness, joy, and anxiety), preferring to focus on men's actions rather than their inner worlds. Yet anger can be a frightening and uncomfortable experience for men, who may fear that their anger will get out of control and result in their hurting someone either physically or emotionally. Or the expression of anger might upset a man's view of himself as a "nice guy."

This chapter is mainly written for men who want to understand and deal with their anger in more effective ways. At the same time, women may find it helpful in understanding the gender-specific aspects of anger in their male partners, or they may see something of themselves in "masculine" patterns of anger, since people's styles of thinking, feeling, and behaving do not always conform to the cultural stereotypes for their sex.

To begin, here are two brief descriptions of men who struggle with ineffective approaches to their anger.

## ✦ *Anthony's Story*

Anthony is an exceptionally bright young man who is determined to "do the right thing" in his life. He wants to work hard, raise a family, go to church, and be respected in the community. He went to college on an academic scholarship, completed his postgraduate work in record time, and holds a good job in a research laboratory. Anthony has only had one girlfriend in his life, Susan, whom he met at age fifteen. They married last year, right after Anthony was awarded his Ph.D. in chemistry. When he talks about Susan, you would think that Anthony is describing a saint or a goddess, not a real person. He seems to sincerely believe that she has no faults and that she knows exactly what each of them should do to achieve the perfect relationship. If he feels differently about something than she does, it is always because he is wrong and she is right.

All is not well with Anthony, however. Although he is a pious, churchgoing person, he harbors an embarrassing secret: he is nearly addicted to Internet pornography. He takes every advantage to view it, unbeknownst to his wife. There are periods of time when he has been able to control his urges, but he has little confidence in his ability to do so long term. A description of one of his recent viewing binges provides some insight into the connection between Anthony's voyeuristic behavior and his deeply buried anger.

The incident occurred a year before Anthony and Susan were married. Anthony was nearly single-mindedly involved in preparing for his doctoral examinations and Susan felt neglected by him during these months of his intense studying. Rather than negotiating for some of his time and attention, as a healthy anger expresser would do, Susan instead criticized Anthony for a number of what she perceived were his faults: that her parents didn't seem to like him as much as she wished, that he was not as physically attractive as she would like, that he chose to start his career in a modestly paying research laboratory instead of in lucrative corporate work, and that he sometimes experiences erectile problems. Susan mused about what her life would have been like had she decided to marry someone else.

Anthony was deeply hurt, but being an intellectual man who was not very aware of his feelings, Anthony experienced his hurt as a kind of physical "buzz" (a vague sense in his gut that something was wrong). He had become adept at ignoring this feeling. Because he believed that Susan could do no wrong, he accepted her criticisms as reasonable. She managed to work all of these comments into their dinner conversation, and none drew any verbal response from Anthony. Susan then left the apartment to play a game in her Wednesday night volleyball league.

About a half hour after Susan had departed, Anthony reached a point in his studying where he realized that he needed to review some information on polymer science available on the Internet. His office had a subscription to the Web site, and since it was only five minutes away, he drove there and entered the empty building. Logging on to his computer, he quickly located the information and began to print thirty pages worth of material. As the pages came out at a rate of about two per minute, Anthony turned to a pornography Web site he knew all too well. He ogled various images of beautiful naked women and viewed them in rapid succession. He became aroused and masturbated, eventually reaching orgasm. Then he looked at the clock and realized that he had been flipping from image to image for nearly ninety minutes.

Anthony thought that he had barely enough time to log off and return home before Susan arrived. But he was wrong. Susan did not come home until 2 A.M. She went out to a bar after the game and spent the evening drinking and flirting with the male players.

Anthony's behavior was a part of a pattern that Anthony later understood with the help of a therapist. Whenever he and Susan experienced conflict, Anthony took the first opportunity to find his way to Internet pornography. But prior to therapy, his behavior seemed only to reflect incidents of particularly intense sexual desire, unconnected to their relationship. For her part, Susan's flirting and provocative criticisms followed the same pattern.

Anthony's story is illustrates one of the great mantras of psychology: "Emotion never lies, and emotion never lies still."

Anthony was deeply hurt; he understandably felt the threat of losing the only woman he had ever loved; and he was angry at Susan's mistreatment of him. But he felt helpless to disagree with her or even to acknowledge his feelings to himself. The only way he knew to deal with the conflict was to have affairs outside of the relationship. He didn't do so literally—he was a shy person who was quite afraid of women—so he did so symbolically through pornography use. His anger avoidance (and Susan's as well) resulted in damage to the relationship and deep-seated feelings of shame. Anthony certainly did not want to use pornography, but he felt that he had no control over himself. He could live the life he intended to live only if he could learn to deal with his feelings and negotiate within his relationship.

Here is another brief case study, on the surface very different from Anthony, but at a deeper level, basically similar.

## ✦ Blair's Story

Blair is a chronically angry person who becomes belligerent at the slightest indication of maltreatment. He is aggressive in traffic, domineering in relationships, and prone to shouting and threatening others. Blair flies into a rage at the drop of a hat, has difficulty getting along with coworkers, and suffers from frequent backaches, stomach problems, and sleep difficulties.

In contrast to Anthony, Blair (clearly an anger exploder), fits the stereotype of men and anger. It is important to acknowledge that men are all different from one another—that there is a wide diversity of personality styles among men. At the same time, stereotypes are revealing—they tell us something about the cultural expectations that affect us all. Although a lot of men are not like Blair or Anthony, every man nonetheless experiences similar social expectations to deal with his feelings "like a man." For a variety of reasons, some men do not buy into masculine stereotypes about anger as fully as men like Blair do. Some are so fearful of their rageful tendencies that they become anger avoiders like Anthony. Others have learned the healthy pattern of the anger expresser.

In order to really understand Anthony's and Blair's problems, you need to understand the way that many men are socialized to deal with anger. Gender (cultural expectations based on your biological sex) provides an important context for many behaviors, especially those connected with the world of feelings. Therefore, if you are to learn healthier ways of dealing with your emotional life, you need to pay attention to this important component of human experience. This chapter describes the cultural forces that influence men's relationship to anger. The hope is to help you cope better with your own issues. First, it is important to assess the extent to which you fit the pattern of masculine anger avoidance. This quiz is written for men, but, as mentioned, some women might have similar patterns of anger avoidance.

# The Masculine Anger Avoidance Quiz

1. Do you feel that the other person in the relationship (wife, girlfriend, partner) is the "relationship expert" and that your opinions are wrong if he or she disagrees with you?

2. Do you find yourself engaging in behaviors that your partner would disapprove of (disparaging him or her when talking to your friends, flirting with others, using pornography) and hiding these behaviors from your partner?

3. In arguments, do you often present yourself as being helpless, saying "I forgot," "I got tied up in something else," or "I'm tired"?

4. Do you sometimes label yourself as a "wimp" or "henpecked"?

5. Do you avoid mentioning your partner in conversations with your male friends, afraid that they might tease you as unmasculine for being too close to or too influenced by her or him?

6. Do you secretly make plans to get away from your partner, to avoid conflict, rather than negotiating for time apart?

7. When arguing with your partner, do you often find yourself trying to explain why his or her position is illogical, thinking that the other person will come around to agree with you if only he or she would be rational?

8. Do you find yourself shutting down emotionally during conflicts?

9. Do you respond to conflict by pouting?

10. Are you prone to using alcohol or other drugs to dull your vulnerable feelings?

If you answered yes to some of these questions, your behavior is typical of the masculine anger avoider in primary relationships. These behaviors reflect the ways that men are taught to deal with emotions and romantic partners. The ability to change these unhealthy patterns rests in part on understanding the gendered pressures on men to think, feel, and act in ways that society defines as masculine.

# Gender As Cultural Pressure

People often use the words *sex* and *gender* interchangeably. Here the word *sex* refers to the biological: hormones, chromosomes, genitalia, secondary sex characteristics, and so on. The term *gender* refers to social behaviors like aggression, conversational style, parenting behaviors, and relational patterns; *masculine* and *feminine* characterize behavior in terms of gender, not sex. Although social behaviors may be influenced by biology, they are also strongly affected by socialization, reward and punishment, situational conditions, and other psychological factors. As discussed in chapter 8, although most masculine people are male, there are also feminine men and masculine women. It is important to remember that sex and gender do not always go together within an individual person.

Nearly everyone has had a conversation about "what's the difference between men and women?" The stereotypes emerge: women will always ask for directions when they're lost in the car, men will never worry about whether their underwear looks pretty, women will always be able to watch a television show for more than ten seconds without reaching for the remote, men never say "I love you," and on and on. (By the way, none of these things are true. When you see the words *always* and *never* in statements about people, you can usually bet that these claims are overgeneralized.) But few people ever have conversations about "what are the similarities between men and women?" or, "what is the diversity among men or among women?" And even when people talk about the differences, you rarely hear them take it to the next step: "What causes these differences?" There is a tendency to just accept the differences at face value, or perhaps there is an implicit assumption that biology is the culprit. At any rate, people seem to generally assume that behavioral dissimilarities exist between men and women in nearly every social sphere, and that these dissimilarities are immutable.

Research tells us otherwise. It turns out that men and women have much more common ground than they have differences, and that there is great variation within the populations of each sex. If biology holds behavior on a leash, it is a very long and loose one. More than any other animal, human beings are creatures of experience. The distinction between sex and gender is important because if you believe that men and women behave in the ways that they do because of their sex, there isn't much you can do about it; biological evolution takes thousands of years. But if you understand that social forces are preeminent in shaping human behavior, you can be much more hopeful about the possibility of transforming the limiting effect of (some aspects of) gender on your ability to cope with the world. Social evolution is a slow process, but its speed is blinding when compared with the snail's pace of biological transformation, and individual change can be much faster than that. If you consider some aspects of gender to be damaging, the understanding that they are strongly influenced by environmental factors gives hope for exerting control over problems through changing the social forces that give rise to them.

The bottom line is that sex doesn't change much, but gender does. You can see shifts in gender recently taking place, for example, in the increased participation of girls in organized sports, in a fivefold increase within a decade in the number of full-time male homemakers ("househusbands"), in changes in the sex composition of the labor force, in sex integration of previously single-sex institutions or professions, in the increase in lesbian and gay adoption, and in social movements designed to redefine what it means to be a man, woman, father, or mother. Gender varies historically and cross-culturally. A man can learn new skills that will help him make his way in the world of gender and relationships, despite the fact that he has been told for years that it is impossible or undesirable to do so.

Gender is a set of cultural forces that influence people to behave, experience the self, and experience the world in characteristic ways based on the biological categorization of male and female. However, it is critical to understand that individuals' reactions to this cultural pressure are widely variable—we all know women who like sports and men who do not, men who are emotional and women who are not, women with little interest in children and men with a lot of interest in children. Some people conform in lockstep to masculine and feminine ideologies, some resist every gendered dictate, and most people react in ways that are somewhere in between these two extremes. If you feel like you are not a "typical" man, rest assured that individual variation is more the rule than the exception.

An understanding of gender is critical to the understanding of anger because the culture prescribes very gendered ways of dealing with anger. If the pressure to handle anger in certain ways is embedded in the pressure to experience the gendered self in certain ways, then you must deal with the gendered context of the problem. It is very difficult to resist a pressure that you cannot name, and most men spend very little time reflecting on the pressure to behave and experience themselves in ways that society deems appropriate for males.

Men are all different, but the one thing men share is the cultural pressure to be masculine. If you uncritically conform to this social influence, you are at risk for developing problems in handling anger. If you can learn to understand and resist cultural masculinity at the times when it is important to do so, you can transform yourself from an unhealthy anger exploder or avoider into a healthy anger expresser.

# Masculinity and Antifemininity

The cultural pressure for men to behave and experience themselves in ways that are defined as sex-appropriate comes from many sources: parents, the media, peer groups, community traditions, and organized religion, to name only a few. In mainstream culture, the core of masculinity is *antifemininity*: the disdain for females and feminine behavior. Boys learn early in their lives that the worst insult is the suggestion that a boy throws, runs, acts, talks, or looks like a girl. *Homophobia*, the hatred and fear of gay males, is in part a derivative of antifemininity. After all, what could be more feminine than loving a man? In boyhood and even in adult male peer groups, high-status males use antifemininity and homophobia to enforce conformity to masculine standards of behavior. For instance, a boy gets hurt in a neighborhood game of touch football and he feels like crying. If he does, the other boys are likely to call him a sissy or otherwise shame him. When boys are labeled as girly or gay, they lose status with their male friends, sometimes to the point of being completely ostracized from the group. Therefore, they learn to bring their behavior into line with the expectations for masculinity in the group. You may remember incidents from your childhood, or even from your adult life, when you went to great lengths to avoid feeling or being labeled feminine.

Antifemininity is socialized into males when they are boys and enforced in interactions among many adult men. For instance, when a male golfer leaves a long putt well short of the hole, he is sometimes called "Alice," or people say he "got his putter tangled up in his skirt." Such a pronouncement is made in jest, but it nevertheless reflects the ideologies that women are weaker than men and thus defective and that men demonstrate their masculine value by avoiding behaviors and feelings associated with women. It also fosters men's contempt of women, which makes it harder for heterosexual men to have successful intimate relationships with women.

Antifemininity goes well beyond these relatively trivial golf course interactions. Corporate men who opt for parental leave may jeopardize their potential for advancement within the organization because the men in power hold a prejudiced view of how men should deal with family issues. Men who are interested in becoming elementary school teachers are suspected of pedophilia. People are less likely to vote for male political candidates who act in feminine ways. Men who are influenced by their wives or girlfriends are disparaged as "whipped" or "henpecked."

# Antifemininity and Behavior

Antifemininity is a powerful cultural force that impels gender-conforming men to exert considerable time and energy into proving that they don't have an ounce of femininity in their bodies. Masculinity is defined as a negative essence (being not-like-a-woman), and it is impossible to prove a negative. Perhaps you stood up to a bigger or more powerful guy today, but does that mean that you will do so tomorrow? This negative essence accounts for the seemingly insane behaviors that characterize hypermasculinity.

Take a look at perhaps the most stereotypical one: refusing to ask for directions when you're lost. Is it that this man, in his heart of hearts, really wants to find that place on his own? Not at all. In fact, if his wife or girlfriend is with him and she is willing to ask for directions, he will readily accept the information. He doesn't ask because requesting help is defined as something that women do, and therefore he is motivated to avoid doing so. He could be a much more efficient and effective problem solver if he would just behave in a culturally defined feminine way. Other stereotypical masculine behaviors (refusing to cry when in emotional or physical pain, downplaying your emotional connection to a wife or girlfriend, pushing yourself beyond exhaustion in work or athletics, or even running in front of stampeding bulls) are attempts to prove that you are not feminine.

Men who accept masculine ideology in uncritical ways find themselves compulsively attempting to prove what is essentially unprovable. One Native American tribe refers to masculinity as "The Big Impossible."

Central to the definition of masculinity are dictates about dominance, control, and independence. A man is supposed to be in command of himself, "his woman," other men, and his feelings. He goes after what he wants, never takes no for an answer, is detached from the "entanglements" of intimate relationships, uses violence or the threat of violence if necessary, and never displays, as the old handbook of the Virginia Military Institute says, "fear, hate, embarrassment, ardor, or hilarity." Men are expected to constrain any vulnerable feelings or indications that they are emotionally connected to others. Men who refuse to conform are accused of not being "real men" or not being "red-blooded men," as if emotional expression relegated men to the realm of unreality or changed the color of their blood.

# Masculinity and Emotion

A popular T-shirt displays the slogan "No Fear," as if fear were a poison or a disease. This saying is emblematic of a central masculine cultural dictate: When faced with vulnerable emotion, marshal your abilities to move your discomfort as far away from your experience as is humanly (or perhaps inhumanly) possible, even to the point of denying that the feeling even exists. The highest masculine value is control over your vulnerable emotions, and gender-conforming men learn all too well how to send the world of feeling to an underground compartment buried deep within their psyches.

Curiously, the culture does not prescribe masculine control for two specific kinds of emotional experiences in men: anger and lust. We expect men to be sexually interested in women, and we tend to think that anger is a natural part of a man's world. In contrast to the vulnerable emotions, which are supposed to be in a man's complete control, anger and lust are seen as completely out of control. If a man feels fear or sentimentality, he is supposed to shut it down, but if he feels anger or sexual arousal, it's a runaway train.

Obviously, the focus of this book is on anger, but a brief mention of masculine lust may provide an instructive parallel. Masculine lust is seen as out of control in a *behavioral* sense. In other words, if an attractive woman offers herself sexually to a man, he is expected to accept that offer, regardless of whether or not he has an understanding of sexual exclusivity with another woman. At the same time, masculine lust is not out of control emotionally. In erotic novels or heterosexual pornography films, the descriptions and portrayals of sexual activity nearly always center around women's pleasure (the emotion) and men's performance (the behavior). Men are rarely depicted as attached, moaning with pleasure, saying how good they feel, or even smiling. In fact, it is unclear what they feel, if anything. They grunt occasionally, they thrust incessantly, and they sweat profusely, but rarely does the reader or viewer get any kind of indication about what is going on inside of the man. Physiologically, he must be aroused (*impotence* literally means "powerlessness," an unmasculine trait if ever there was one), but he must also be in control of his body, lest he reach orgasm before he has "satisfied the woman," and in control of his feelings, lest he become too attached to her to retain his masculine independence. And he must direct the sexual action; many of these descriptions romanticize male dominance. Even the supposedly out-of-control experience of sexual desire includes aspects of a tight grip on the emotional reins.

# Masculinity, Anger, and Violence

In a way, the control dimension of anger is similar to that of lust, but in another way it is not. The similarity is that men often use anger in an instrumental way. An anger exploder can so frighten his coworkers or romantic partner that they readily conform their behavior to his desires, and therefore the expression of his anger is in the service of exerting dominance over other people, at least in the short term. At the extreme is the most common type of domestic violence perpetrator, often referred to as the "power and control" type. He flies into rages and uses physical violence or the threat of it to coerce his partner into doing what he wants her to do. Because of the perception of anger as being out of control for men, the batterer often uses his feelings as a justification for his irresponsibility—"I hit her because I was angry"—or he assigns responsibility to the partner: "She *made* me mad."

He never acknowledges the vulnerable feelings beneath the anger. He could never say that he hit her because he was sad, ashamed, or worried. And he never accepts responsibility for his behavior. (One aspect of batterer treatment is to dispel the myth of being out of control by pointing out to perpetrators that they make decisions all during the violent episodes, for example, by hitting her with an open hand instead of a fist, pushing her onto the bed instead of the floor, or hitting the wall instead of hitting her. The goal is to hold them responsible for their behavior instead of blaming their victims or their allegedly out-of-control feelings.)

The dissimilarity between cultural dictates around anger and lust is that, when it comes to anger, there is a cultural pressure for men to reveal their internal states, in sharp contrast to every other experience of feeling. Unfortunately, the masculine emotional manifestation of anger is often rage, and the behavioral manifestation is often violence or some other form of victimization. In the United States, males account for 86 percent of all violent crimes, and there are now over a million men in federal and state prisons paying a heavy price for failing to resist the toxic ideologies of mainstream cultural masculinity (Greenfield and Snell 1999).

But anger is not violence, contrary to what many men believe. In the movies, or perhaps even in your family of origin or childhood peer group, when someone got angry, violence seemed appropriate. But there are better ways of understanding anger and better skills for dealing with it.

# Experiencing, Labeling, and Displaying Anger

Psychologist Ronald Levant refers to anger as the male "emotional funnel system" (1995, 240). Since all men have feelings regardless of whether they want to or not, and since anger is the only emotion that is deemed socially appropriate for men to experience and display, there is a tendency among some men to convert any and all emotional experiences into anger. Feeling anxious, jealous, sad, embarrassed, or ashamed, these men tend to display nothing but anger. You see the justification of this emotional funnel system again and again on television and at the movies. A man's wife or friend is hurt or killed, but masculine men are not supposed to experience vulnerable emotions like sadness and grief—the natural reactions to psychological losses. Instead, they can only experience anger, and they do not react by merely feeling, they must also react by doing, which usually translates into hunting down and hurting or killing the perpetrator, thus doubling the amount of violence that takes place.

Recent research indicates that people who view a lot of media violence such as this—violence that seems justified—are more likely to become physically aggressive than those who tend to abstain from viewing these kinds of stories (Huesmann et al. 2003). There is a social script that follows a common pathway: victimization, conversion of all feelings into anger, and perpetration of violence. To make matters worse, usually some kind of social reward, such as "getting the girl," follows the violence, and there is little exploration of the long-term physical, emotional, or financial costs of this behavior. People learn that violence is masculine and justified, and that it is an effective way to solve problems. Some children's television programming (such as *Teenage Mutant Ninja Turtles*, *Mighty Morphin Power Rangers*, and *Road Runner* cartoons) even display the violence as fun.

Many boys learn early in their lives that they are to eschew vulnerable feelings and experience in favor of seemingly empowering feeling and action. Between birth and age forty months, boys (on the average) actually display more indications of emotionality than girls. But between ages forty and sixty months, the pattern reverses, coincident with a period of rapid language development. One explanation for this may lie in parent-child interactions.

Parents tend to use emotional vocabulary with their daughters but not their sons. When a girl comes home and tells her parents that other children are being unkind to her, parents often ask her how it makes her feel—sad? worried? But a boy who approaches his parents with the same complaint is much more likely to be asked, "What are you going to *do* about it?" Thus, parents (often unconsciously) communicate to girls that feelings are important and to boys that feelings are not important at all, especially if they are vulnerable emotions. In a somewhat stereotypical interaction, a boy begins to cry and his father says threateningly, "*I'll* give you something to cry about!" He learns not only that vulnerable feelings are to be avoided; he also learns that they are dangerous.

You may recall incidents from your childhood in which your parents or other adults gave you messages about how boys should deal with emotions in general or anger in particular. Mainstream culture doesn't teach boys the words that they can use to access and label their feelings. We orient them so much to the external world that they never develop the ability to understand and deal with what is inside.

Research also indicates that boys are physically punished more often than girls, and that fathers are more likely than mothers to administer the punishment. And so boys disproportionately experience violence at the hands of their fathers, and they may learn important lessons in the process. First, they learn the aforementioned connection between anger and action. Second, they learn that violence is what men do when their anger gets out of control. And they learn that fathers are fearsome creatures who compel obedience through the threat of physical aggression. If they grow up uncritically accepting these lessons, they are likely to replay the pattern of abuse with their own children, especially if these children are boys. Research indicates that, among survivors of childhood abuse, those who fail to label their experience as abusive are much more likely to be perpetrators of violence than those who describe their victimization as abnormal, as the following case illustrates.

### ✦ Roy's Story

Roy is a forty-four-year-old father of three boys. When he was young, his father repeatedly and severely punished him for even minor infractions of the house rules. These punishments typically took the form of whippings with his father's belt, and on occasion, Roy's father would slap him or even hit him in his face or stomach with a closed fist. Roy grew up fearing his father but also identifying with him. He perceived the beatings as obviously painful but also as normal and necessary. After all, this was the only father he knew; there was nobody to compare him with. When he was very young, Roy would cry when he was whipped, but when he got older, he learned how to keep himself from crying, a "skill" that his younger brother could never manage. Whenever Roy and his brother were beaten at the same time, Roy's father would tell his brother that he was a sissy and that he should be more like Roy—taking his "medicine" like a man. After Roy became an adult, a friend once asked him if his father had ever whipped him when he was young, and Roy replied, "Yes, sir. And it's the best thing he ever did for me. I deserved it, and it showed me how to be a man."

Thus, Roy not only accepted his abuse, he also romanticized it and identified more closely with the feelings of his father, the aggressor, than he did with himself, the victim. Not surprisingly, Roy also routinely beats his own sons and associates the squelching of vulnerable feeling with being masculine. He sincerely believes that his violence is doing his sons a favor because it will result in healthy development. His sons live in constant fear of him, just as Roy lived in fear of his father. Review your own history of punishment, especially at the hands of your father or other adult males. What messages did the form and pattern of punishments convey?

Returning to the case presented at the beginning of this chapter, you find a similar parental role model in Anthony's life. His father was also an angry, physically punitive, and emotionally abusive man. But in contrast to Roy, Anthony does not identify with his father. He hates him, and long ago he vowed that he would never be like him. So when Anthony gets angry, for him it means that he is like his father, and his reaction is one of deep self-hatred and shame—self-hatred for being like his father and shame for having been unworthy of his father's love. Anthony knows that he does not want to be like his violent father, but he know no other alternative than to banish his anger from his experience. Prior to entering psychotherapy, he had never articulated his feelings about his father or about himself, either to another person or to himself.

# Boys and Bullying

Male peer groups often engage in physical bullying and other forms of aggression. Thus many sons of abusive fathers suffer victimization from more than one male source. Indeed, male-to-male aggression is so common that it is frequently not even defined as problematic. Nonetheless, many adult males are indeed survivors of physical abuse from one source or another. Identifying (self-labeling) yourself as a survivor is an important step in recovering from abuse, and, as mentioned earlier, unacknowledged survivors are more likely than acknowledged survivors to become perpetrators of further violence. To what extent are you a survivor of physical or emotional maltreatment from male peers or adults?

# Survivors, Masculinity, and Anger Explosion

Psychologist David Lisak (1996) provides another important piece of the puzzle with regard to men, survival of abuse, anger, and violence in his research on adult male perpetration of serious violence. He notes that violent men are overwhelmingly likely to have been victims of severe violence as children. They are also very likely to uncritically accept social definitions of masculinity as violent and unfeeling. It is as if, Lisak says, there were two routes that survivors of severe abuse take. They can acknowledge the vulnerable feelings associated with their traumatic experiences, in which case they are prone to conventional mental health problems, such as anxiety disorders or depression. Or they can seal over their pain by accepting masculine dictates to control their feelings, in which case they act out their pain by being violent toward others. Anger explosion for men may well be a part of this formula: childhood victimization in some form, combined with acceptance of toxic masculine ideologies, reinforced and modeled by family, media, and peers.

# Survivors and Anger Avoidance

And yet many men do not become anger exploders. Instead, they become anger avoiders, perhaps because they are so frightened by masculine manifestations of rage and violence that they exert considerable energy to contain their anger before it gets out of control. Many fathers understandably worry, "Could I lose control and hit my own children in the same way that my father beat me?" They are fearful that if they get angry, they will behave violently.

If men habitually use anger to deflect their feelings from other emotions that they consider unmasculine, then anger itself may become threatening because, consciously or unconsciously, it signals these other more vulnerable and "feminine" feelings. Because it signals vulnerable emotion, their anger is accompanied by strong feelings of shame. They have internalized the other males in their histories who beat them up emotionally and physically for displaying human feelings, and so they have learned to beat themselves up. It is as if the fathers and the bullies are right there in the room with them. It appears that the man who is most prone to the anger avoidance pattern is the one that used to be called "thin-skinned," the man who is easily hurt, who takes a long time to get over an incident in which he feels mistreated. His hurt often manifests itself as pouting and brooding. He has lots of feelings but few skills to manage them.

Because the voices inside of him say that emotions are unmasculine, the anger avoider keeps his feelings to himself. His sensitivity, which is a potential strength, is instead guarded as "the big secret." And if someone gets too close to him (as is inevitable in his primary relationship), his partner might discover his shame and his secret. Then he finds himself not only avoiding the emotion, but the relationship as well. Sadness, worry, and sentimentality do not feel safe, and because anger is stimulated by these experiences, it does not feel safe either. Therefore, it only feels safe to stay away from all emotions.

# The Surfacing of Emotion

Feeling safe is not the same as being safe. Again, anger is a normal part of life, and it is inevitable that people deal with it either directly or indirectly. When people do not handle anger directly, it leaks out, sometimes in very inappropriate ways. Anger-avoiding men who accept masculine ideologies may exhibit several patterns of behavior that are damaging to themselves or to their relationships with others. Here are some of the behaviors they may manifest:

**Substance abuse.** Men are twice as likely as women to have unhealthy substance use patterns, especially with regard to the most abused drug in the world, alcohol. Drinking heavily allows a man to dull his feelings by dulling his consciousness, or it may give him permission to express his vulnerable feelings and later dismiss his behavior by saying that it was "just the beer talking."

**Relationship infidelity.** When angry with their romantic partners and unable to express their feelings or negotiate in their relationships, men can punish their partners by being sexually unfaithful. They may rationalize their behavior by believing that they were carried away by lust. Recall Anthony's indirect expression of this pattern described at the beginning of this chapter.

**Stereotyping women.** In conflicts with their female partners, men are faced with seemingly incongruent feelings. They love their partners and yet they become angry with them at the same time. They can resolve this apparent paradox by believing that *all* women do what their particular partners do. Then they can complain about women in general, thereby displacing the source of their dissatisfaction.

**Emotional stonewalling.** Men can punish their partners by sulking or becoming uncommunicative, thus increasing interpersonal distance and justifying the behavior by appealing to masculine independence.

**Complaining to others.** Men can deal with their frustration with their female partners by having "bitching" sessions with other men. It is interesting to listen to the language they use in these complaints. Rarely do they refer to their wives by their first names, instead using "my wife" (a possession), or "the wife" (an object, and a denial of the connection with her), or even "the old ball and chain" (a burden).

**Psychophysiological symptoms.** The suppression of emotion is associated with a wide variety of physical problems, including cardiovascular disorders, gastrointestinal problems, backaches, headaches, sleep difficulties, and even skin disorders.

# The Threat behind the Anger

You have already seen that anger is usually a reaction to threat, and you can apply this model to a gender-aware understanding of masculine anger. Anger can be a response to a number of gender-specific threats.

**Loss of dominance or control.** Masculine men are supposed to be in control of themselves at all times and to never allow another person to dominate them. As with most requirements of gender, this is asking the impossible. Men who accept traditional gender ideologies may feel threatened when another person is in charge or when they find it difficult or impossible to direct a situation.

**Sexual attractiveness or inadequacy.** Part of being in control is controlling your partner's attraction. Men who feel inadequate often convert this feeling into a jealousy that drives them to restrict their partners' lives. For instance, there are men who want to know where their wives or girlfriends are at all times or who try to narrow their partners' circle of friends or other social contacts. They become enraged at any sign of their partners' independence. This strategy is self-defeating, as it often causes women to want to end the relationship. Sexual inadequacy can also be experienced as a threat. Periodic erectile dysfunction is a very common experience, especially as men age. The man who expects himself to perform sexually in the same way he did in his twenties, and who is unable to deal with disappointment or grief, may convert these feelings into anger.

**Possible pain and injury.** Sports are the great training ground for masculinity, and men and boys can incorporate *metamessages* (ideas of how you should handle yourself in general) from situations in sports. For example, nearly every fight that takes place in athletics results from a similar situation: one player thinks that another player is trying to harm him. He and his teammates respond with a "preemptive strike"—threatening or enacting violence so that they will not be injured or dominated. Perhaps it is important to confront intimidation in a sporting contest, but refusing to back down in the real world can have dire consequences, as in incidents of road rage (over 95 percent of participants in this type of violence are men). At the same time, anger at being mistreated is legitimate, and anger avoiders suffer negative consequences when they cannot deal with their feelings safely and effectively.

**Dependence or neediness.** Masculinity tells men that they must not ever be dependent or needy, but these are natural and universal human states. When men want to be nurtured but feel unmasculine in expressing this desire, they may convert their feelings into anger. You see the extreme of this problem in men whose partners leave them. Feeling dependent, needy, and lonely, but at the same time finding these experiences unacceptable, many men instead respond with violence, substance abuse, or some other form of acting out, none of which helps them with the grief process that naturally ensues after an important loss.

**Feeling unappreciated.** Because many men have been taught that nothing they do is ever good enough, they may not be good at appreciating their own work in the context of their occupations, parenting, or primary relationships. Because they have not developed the ability to care for themselves, they may expect others to do it for them and feel resentful during those inevitable times when a boss, child, or partner fails to say "thank you."

# Men's Gendered Struggles

The work in this section owes much to discussions with my good friend and colleague, Linda LaFave, who also graciously reviewed an earlier draft of the entire chapter, and also to my conversations with John Lynch.

Solutions to anger avoidance are found throughout this book. This chapter focuses on the gendered context of men's anger, and understanding this context will lead to a more sophisticated approach toward the goal of becoming a healthy anger expresser. To review, it is important to remember that all men are different. At the same time, there are a number of things that many men tend not to be very good at doing:

**Identifying vulnerable emotions.** Because anger is the masculine "emotional funnel system," many men experience only anger and have little awareness of the vulnerable feelings associated with it.

**Grieving.** When you undergo a significant loss (death of a friend or a family member, a relationship breakup, the loss of a job, the onset of health problems, and so on), you must psychologically reorganize your sense of self to include the fact that the loss has occurred. The grief process includes sadness, reminiscing, anger, crying, wishing that things had been different, and wondering what you could have done to avoid or delay the loss. Many men are poor at grieving because it involves several experiences and activities that they consider unmasculine, like experiencing vulnerable feelings, revealing themselves to another person, and allowing spontaneous expressions of emotion to surface. As a result, they may experience a variety of symptoms: sleeplessness, heavy drinking, distractibility, and undirected anger, among others. Their bodies and brains are telling them that they need to grieve, but they do not believe it, and they do not know how to do it. When asked, "In what way do you think counseling can help you?" they often answer, "I want you to help me not think about it."

**Learning about gender.** Few men read or talk to others about their experiences with gender socialization or the social pressure to behave in ways that society defines as masculine. They experience gender pressure as "just the way it is." Thus they have no language with which to understand masculinity or to resist its toxic aspects. It is very difficult to resist a pressure that you cannot name, and so they are unaware that they can behave and experience themselves in different ways from cultural dictates. And most men feel like misfits in the face of impossible demands to always be sure of themselves and never experience negative emotions. Because they do not talk to other men about their "unmasculine" inner life, it is carried as the shameful "big secret."

**Paying attention to emotions.** As noted earlier, males are deflected away from using words that are descriptive of feelings, beginning at an early age. For some men, the question, "how do you feel?" does not even make sense, and they have difficulty distinguishing their feelings from their thoughts. If asked how he feels about his girlfriend leaving, a man who has difficulty knowing his feelings might respond, "I feel she shouldn't have done it." In some traditional heterosexual relationships, the man succeeds for the woman and the woman emotes for the man. In some cases, she knows how he is feeling before he does. To use a golfing analogy, the woman is the man's emotional caddy. Because gender pressures focus on men's thoughts and actions rather than on their inner experiences, many men fail to develop an emotional vocabulary. They experience feelings as a nonspecific bodily sensation, or "buzz," but have great difficulty identifying the character or the source of this sensation.

**Being relational.** Because men have been taught from an early age to be independent and self-sufficient, they often lack relationship skills. For men in contemporary culture, this problem is compounded by the American romantic myth that happy relationships are merely a matter of meeting the right person—that if you find "the one," your life will be wonderful without any adjustment or effort on your part.

**Respecting women.** Males are often encouraged to have contempt for women and to see women as weak and in need of protection. Stereotypical chivalry actually stems from the belief that men need to take care of women at all times, even doing things that women are quite capable of doing themselves, such as opening a door or filling a wine glass. Chivalric men often feel that they have to fix any problem that a woman has, and so they tend to offer solutions to women who merely want to express their feelings. They also tend to want to rescue women but at the same time may resent doing so.

# Toward Solutions

To include a gendered context to your efforts to become a healthy anger expresser, begin by thinking about the extent to which the problems listed above apply to you. Below are some specific pieces of advice for how to address the anger avoidance associated with each of these struggles.

**Identify the threat behind the anger.** Is the threat related to your feelings about yourself as a man? Such threats may arise from a variety of sources: being dominated, ignored, or confronted, questioning your sexuality or masculinity, stimulating your fears and doubts, undermining your manly image, or challenging your competence. Once you are able to identify the gendered aspect of the threat, you can sort out which part of your anger is due to masculine insecurity (which all men have) and which part of it is a legitimate reaction to being mistreated. Then you can express your anger in a healthy way and negotiate for what you want in the relationship.

**Learn how to grieve.** As noted above, people need to grieve after important losses. Grieving is a natural process; your psyche knows how to do it. If you are having trouble doing it, it is because you are fighting this natural process. And, as noted, many men engage themselves in fighting against grief because it involves experiences and behaviors that are culturally defined as unmasculine. Grieving simply involves allowing yourself to experience the variety of feelings associated with loss—sadness, anxiety, anger, reminiscence—and expressing those feelings in a safe and healthy way. One activity that many men know how to do is to tell stories. If you are used to entertaining others with storytelling, try adapting this mode of expression to grief by highlighting the emotional issues involved in your story. Grieving cannot take place all at once. There are times when you will go for hours or even days without thinking about your loss, and then it will surface again spontaneously. The task is deceptively simple: when you feel, allow yourself to stay with the feeling, and find some way of expressing it, by talking with a close friend, having a make-believe dialogue with people involved in the loss, or writing about your grief experience. Of course, you can also join a grief support group or enlist the aid of a therapist.

**Educate yourself about masculinity.** Regardless of the extent to which you resist or conform to it, gender assumptions provide an important context for people's lives, the default options that the culture pressures you to adopt. For men, many of the dictates of dominant masculinity are psychologically and physically dangerous: don't feel, treat women as objects, don't get too close to anybody, evaluate your self-worth through money, physical strength, and sexual conquest, ignore your pain, and so forth. Because it is very difficult to resist a pressure that you cannot name, it is tremendously empowering to acquire a language with which to understand masculinity. You can do this by reading, discussing gender issues within relationships, taking a class on men and masculinity, or joining a gender-awareness men's group. When gender demands lead to conscious choices, many things become possible.

**Learn to identify feelings and label them verbally.** This skill is discussed elsewhere in this book, so there is no need to belabor it. Suffice it to say that developing an emotional vocabulary is an essential step toward dealing with feelings of all kinds. Many men have difficulty distinguishing between thoughts and feelings. This is an important skill, and as with any skill, it improves with practice.

**Develop relationship skills.** Learn how to listen to people's complaints and problems and offer support without trying to fix the problem for them. Be honest about your own needs and learn how to communicate your desires. Ask for what you want in a relationship and negotiate for it. The constructive and appropriate expression of anger in a relationship is as important an intimacy skill as being romantic and thoughtful. If you want to have a good relationship, you will have to learn how to let your partner know what is taking place inside of you, even if it makes both of you uncomfortable for a time. Initially, you may be ashamed of revealing the "unmasculine" side of you, but soon you will experience this activity as freeing and empowering, as it allows you to be who you truly are. Doing what is important, despite the fact that it is defined as unmasculine, is not "weak," but instead indicates real strength and resolve.

**Learn about sexism.** Learn about the difference between chivalry and respect, and apply it to your own life. Chivalry is the application of a rigid set of rules for interactions with women, based on the mistaken belief that all women are exactly the same. Respect for a woman involves taking the time to get to know her, putting yourself in her place (being empathic), allowing her to be different from you, acknowledging her feelings, and according her values, beliefs, and desires a status equal to your own. Everybody wants respect; not everybody wants chivalry.

# Expanding Masculinity

Becoming a healthy anger expresser does not mean that you must completely discard cultural masculinity. Rather, it involves a resistance to the destructive aspects and an expansion of the healthy aspects of traditional masculinity. So in closing, here are some positive cultural ideals for men and ways to expand your thinking about them.

+ *Courage* is taking a risk because you are committed to the outcome. It is different from *bravado*, which is taking a risk so that others will not think you are a coward. Courage is about what you feel a need to do, whereas bravado is about how you want others to think of you.

Many men define courage only in physical terms, such as running into a burning building to save someone. But you can expand your understanding of courage into the emotional and relational realm. It is courageous to take a psychological risk by expressing your feelings, asking for what you want, and talking about masculinity in the face of cultural pressure to deny your feelings, get what you want through domination, and uncritically accept the culturally dominant definition of masculinity.

✦ *Independence* is freedom of action. It means that you do what is important for you rather than conforming to others' opinions. *Counterdependence* or *oppositionalism* is resisting another person's influence merely to avoid the feeling of being dominated. Although men think of themselves as independent, there is a great deal of conformity to masculine ideologies, behaviors, and attitudes, especially within all-male social groups. Men can be independent, when there is good reason to resist, by not always doing what other men do.

✦ *Loyalty* is being faithful to a person to whom you have made a commitment. For many men, loyalty seems to mean that "anything my buddy does is okay with me." But if your friend is doing something destructive, self-injurious, or disrespectful, it is disloyal not to confront him. And if other men say things that stimulate your legitimate anger (such as sexist or racist remarks), you can be loyal to yourself by challenging these statements.

✦ *Leadership* is using your positive influence to change the direction of a group. Men can be leaders by showing other men healthier visions of masculinity and effective ways of dealing with anger.

✦ *Assertiveness* is claiming your rights as a dignified human being. Men can assert their rights to have feelings, to express those feelings, to behave outside of dominant definitions of gender, and to ask for what they want in relationships.

✦ *Facing a challenge* is getting something done despite the fact that it is difficult. You can face the challenge of building the skills that you have not acquired because cultural masculinity conspired against you. You can accept the challenge to learn how to better relate to others, respect women, take care of your health, access the soft side of your psyche, and deal effectively with your anger. These skills may seem impossible at first, but do you remember the first time you swung a golf club, dribbled a basketball, played a scale on the piano, or solved a crossword puzzle? These activities felt remarkably awkward at first, but if you stuck with them, you probably got so good at them that they soon became second nature. So it is with the skill of healthy anger expression.

# 10

# maintaining the change:
# what to expect

You have read a lot of information about anger, whether it's been in the form of avoiding, exploding, or expressing. You've looked at how your patterns of avoiding or exploding have affected your life in limiting or harmful ways, and you may have made a commitment to change unhealthy patterns into healthy patterns. Great! But which patterns do you know more about, and have more practice and experience with, healthy or unhealthy patterns? It you picked up this book and read it, you probably have more experience and practice with unhealthy patterns than with healthy ones. And when you are not working hard to change your behavior, not paying attention to how you are responding or feeling, or are distracted by confusing or complex interactions, which patterns will slowly or quietly slip back into your behavioral repertoire? Probably it will be the old, familiar, and unhealthy patterns that will creep back in. It's not a matter of *if* these patterns will reemerge but *when* and what you will do when they reappear. Relapse is not a sign of defeat or failure. Rather it is a signal to remember what you've learned and reemploy the skills and ideas you have worked so hard to learn.

Making major changes in your lifestyle is difficult and takes time, patience, and practice. You like to think that you make a change and that's it. You like to think that once you make a change it stays changed. Most often that's not the case. What's worse, thinking that you shouldn't regress once you've committed yourself to a change makes it more difficult and defeating when you run into trouble. You can easily feel defeated by your own habits and familiar behaviors.

The change process is actually more progressive than abrupt, and in order to maintain and continue to grow in the changes you make, you need to plan for and know what to do with relapses and slips. And you need to know how to read your own road signs. When you understand your relapse process, recognize your road signs, and know how to recover from slips, you actually enter a different phase of the process. You will learn not just how to make a change but how to maintain it. This is an important step. You need to be able to maintain the changes you make, or your efforts will lead to defeat and a sense of failure, so eventually you will stop trying. What a shame that would be, especially after all the effort that went into the process so far!

# The Relapse Process

When you make initial changes, you experience new feelings and outcomes. These outcomes may be better than the old ones, but you may not be as familiar with them and may slowly regress back to the old and familiar ways. This is a slow, subtle, and sometimes unconscious process. You might begin by ignoring that little headache you get when you go to work and are annoyed by your coworker playing the same loud music. You might begin by being too tired to deal with the kids or your spouse's habit of leaving the living room a mess. You might say to yourself that it's easier to clean it up yourself. You might begin by knowing that you are feeling angry about a family member's constant calls during dinner but choose to ignore the conflict. There are thousands of ways to begin a relapse. Having a relapse doesn't mean that you've changed all of your behavior back to anger avoider patterns, but the slide is beginning, and it's important that you recognize the pattern. When it happens, talk with your partner, spouse, friends, or other people in your life. Ask them to help you spot a relapse. It is usually the case that people around you will recognize a relapse before you do. It's okay to ask for help. You can't do everything by yourself.

To prepare for the possibility of a relapse, you might want to write a list of the behaviors or patterns you think you would most likely begin to slip into. Make a list now, since your changes are new and more noticeable to you.

1. What are the behaviors that you can now most clearly notice that were part of the trouble for you?

2. What kind of conflict did you tend to avoid?

3. With whom were you most uncomfortable addressing conflict and expressing your anger?

4. What kind of feelings did you use to have more difficulty recognizing?

5. What feelings did you have the most difficulty expressing?

# Road Signs

Road signs are the onset of the particular symptoms you experience on your way through the relapse process and on your way toward a slip. Refer back to chapter 4, which talked about how you experience physiological sensations of arousal when you are angry. What are yours? Chapter 3 talked about symptoms of anger that appear as psychological, behavioral, or physiological indications of distress. These are all road signs. They are the signals that tell you, "Pay attention, you are nearing the city limits of relapse town; slow down and reassess your behavior and beliefs!" You can think of these symptoms as your unique road signs, printed by you, just for you. Your symptoms pointed the way to understanding that there was a problem. The same symptoms can help you see that you have work to do to readjust your behavior and beliefs and not slide back into patterns of avoidance.

What are your road signs? Again, you may want to go back to chapters 3 and 4 to look for the symptoms you identified as your unique responses to threats, your personal alarm system that alerts you to your own anger, sometimes before you even recognize a threat.

1. What signs will you be able to recognize in the future?

2. What signs will someone else be able to recognize first?

3. Which ones would be hard to recognize when you are tired?

4. Which ones would be hard to recognize when you are distracted or busy?

5. Which ones would be the least noticeable?

6. Which ones would bother you the most?

All these road signs let you know something is amiss, something is wrong. They are your way of letting yourself know that you have begun to slide back into old, familiar, and unhealthy patterns of avoiding conflict and withholding the healthy expression of your anger. They let you know that you are avoiding problems, not solving them.

# Slips

Slips occur when you have fully slipped back into your old habits, hook, line, and sinker. You may become immersed once more in dysfunctional relationships, experiencing your full array of psychological, behavioral, and physical symptoms, and at this point are probably pretty miserable. Slips are a full regression. But don't despair. Everything you've learned is still available to you. Change is just a breath away. Remember that just as you learned to withhold, you also can learn to express. You can have as many relapses and slips as it takes for you to finally get it right. You are getting control of your life now, and your way is the right way for you. So don't let anything get in the way. With each relapse or slip you learn more about what makes you avoid, why you avoid, and what skills you can develop to maintain a healthy lifestyle. You can always go back and reread a chapter in this book and write your exercises again to find what it is that you need to do to express your anger in healthy ways. This isn't an impossible mission or a test where you have to get it right the first time. This is your life, and you can learn to make changes at a rate and pace that is comfortable to you. You're in charge now. You've been limited by these patterns for too long. You can make the changes you need to make now that you are in charge of your life again.

# references

Crawford, Mary, and Rhoda Unger. 1996. *Women and Gender: A Feminist Psychology.* New York: McGraw-Hill.

Greenfield, Lawrence A., and Tracy C. Snell. 1999. *Women offenders.* United States Bureau of Justice Statistics Special Report No. 175688. Washington, D.C.: U.S. Government Printing Office.

Hammonds, Cory. 1992. Hypnotic techniques with trauma survivors. Lecture delivered at the Third Annual Eastern Conference on Dissociation and Multiple Personality Disorder, in Alexandria, Virginia.

Huesmann, L. Rowell, Jessica Moise-Titus, Cheryl-Lynn Podolski, and Leonard D. Eron. 2003. Longitudinal relations between children's exposure to TV violence and their aggressive and violent behavior in young adulthood: 1977–1992. *Developmental Psychology* 39(2):200–221.

Levant, Ronald F. 1995. Toward the reconstruction of masculinity. In *A New Psychology of Men,* edited by R. F. Levant and W. S. Pollack. New York: Basic Books.

Lisak, David. 1996. Pain and perpetration in men abused as children. Society for the Psychological Study of Men and Masculinity (SPSMM) *Bulletin* 1(4):16–17.

Lynch, John, and Christopher Kilmartin. 1999. *The Pain behind the Mask: Overcoming Masculine Depression.* New York: Haworth Press.

Martin, Joseph C. 1982. *No Laughing Matter: Chalk Talks on Alcohol.* San Francisco: Harper.

Polce-Lynch, Mary. 2002. *Boy Talk: How You Can Help Your Son Express His Emotions.* Oakland, Calif.: New Harbinger Publications.

# Some Other
# New Harbinger Titles

*Surviving Your Borderline Parent,* Item 3287 $14.95

*When Anger Hurts, second edition,* Item 3449 $16.95

*Calming Your Anxious Mind,* Item 3384 $12.95

*Ending the Depression Cycle,* Item 3333 $17.95

*Your Surviving Spirit,* Item 3570 $18.95

*Coping with Anxiety,* Item 3201 $10.95

*The Agoraphobia Workbook,* Item 3236 $19.95

*Loving the Self-Absorbed,* Item 3546 $14.95

*Transforming Anger,* Item 352X $10.95

*Don't Let Your Emotions Run Your Life,* Item 3090 $17.95

*Why Can't I Ever Be Good Enough,* Item 3147 $13.95

*Your Depression Map,* Item 3007 $19.95

*Successful Problem Solving,* Item 3023 $17.95

*Working with the Self-Absorbed,* Item 2922 $14.95

*The Procrastination Workbook,* Item 2957 $17.95

*Coping with Uncertainty,* Item 2965 $11.95

*The BDD Workbook,* Item 2930 $18.95

*You, Your Relationship, and Your ADD,* Item 299X $17.95

*The Stop Walking on Eggshells Workbook,* Item 2760 $18.95

*Conquer Your Critical Inner Voice,* Item 2876 $15.95

*The PTSD Workbook,* Item 2825 $17.95

*Hypnotize Yourself Out of Pain Now!,* Item 2809 $14.95

*The Depression Workbook, 2nd edition,* Item 268X $19.95

*Beating the Senior Blues,* Item 2728 $17.95

Call **toll free, 1-800-748-6273,** or log on to our online bookstore at **www.newharbinger.com** to order. Have your Visa or Mastercard number ready. Or send a check for the titles you want to New Harbinger Publications, Inc., 5674 Shattuck Ave., Oakland, CA 94609 Include $4.50 for the first book and 75¢ for each additional book, to cover shipping and handling. (California residents please include appropriate sales tax.) Allow two to five weeks for delivery.

*Prices subject to change without notice.*